MW00338543

1914 – 1938
ARMORED
FIGHTING VEHICLES

GEORGE BRADFORD

STACKPOLE
BOOKS

0 11557 00568 4

Published by
STACKPOLE BOOKS
5067 Ritter Road
Mechanicsburg, PA 17055
www.stackpolebooks.com

Cover design by Wendy A. Reynolds

Printed in the United States of America

10 9 8 7 6 5 4 3 2 1

FIRST EDITION

Library of Congress Cataloging-in-Publication Data

Bradford, George.
   1914–1938 armored fighting vehicles / George Bradford. — 1st ed.
      p. cm. — (AFV plans)
   Includes bibliographical references.
   ISBN 978-0-8117-0568-4
   1. Armored vehicles, Military—History—20th century. 2. Tanks (Military science)—History—20th century. 3. Armored vehicles, Military—Drawings. 4. Tanks (Military science)—Drawings. 1. Title. II. Title: Armored fighting vehicles.
   UG446.5.B662010
   623.7'475—dc22
                              2010031279

CONTENTS

INTRODUCTION

This volume is dedicated to 1/48 and 1/35 scale drawings of armored vehicles from an earlier period than those covered to date. There are a few representations of the first tanks that made history in World War I, and then we follow most of the development between the wars up to about 1938. The drawings are organized in a more or less chronological order, working up through the years and labeled by country.

Detailed and clear refrerence is very hard to come by for some of these earlier vehicles, and only the more common ones are covered here. There were also numerous changes made along the way, which resulted in characteristics that only appeared on a given model.

This is by no means a complete coverage of every vehicle from World War I to World War II, but it will be a great resource for anyone modeling this early period. The ultimate purpose of this book is to try to show plan-view scale drawings of these early vehicles that have been overlooked in the previous eight books in this series. Most of these drawings display 4-view plans, but with some of the smaller vehicles we were able to show five or more views. However, no matter how well the plans are drawn, it will always be necessary to have sufficient photo reference books as well.

Over the years, scale drawings of various armored vehicles have appeared in magazines and books, but never all in one place where they would be easy for the researcher or modeler to access them. Many different scales have fought for the limelight, but the more popular ones of late have boiled down to mainly 1/35, 1/48, and 1/72 in the armor modeling world.

You will also find a chart at the beginning of this book for reducing or enlarging any of these drawings to other popular scales. The quality and accuracy of modern photocopying should make it possible for you to achieve whatever final scale you require at the lower end of 1/48 and under. However, in some cases where higher enlargement is required, you may find a certain degree of roughness.

These drawings have been created using vector based drawing applications with line weights ranging from .25 point to 1 point, and thus should easily hold the finer detail when copying. The bulk of these drawings were done over a period of ten years and are currently among the most precise and accurate AFV drawings available. You will also notice a variance in the drawings as the art style changes slightly over the years, but eventually supports shading in the majority of the later works.

SCALE CONVERSIONS

REDUCING

1:72 to 1:76 Scale = 95%

1:48 to 1:72 Scale = 66%

1:48 to 1:76 Scale = 63%

1:48 to 1:87 Scale = 55%

1:48 to 1:87 Scale = 55%

1:35 to 1:48 Scale = 73%

1:35 to 1:76 Scale = 46%

1:35 to 1:72 Scale = 49%

1:35 to 1:87 Scale = 41%

ENLARGING

1:72 to 1:35 Scale = 207%

1:72 to 1:48 Scale = 150%

1:72 to 1:16 Scale = 450%

1:48 to 1:35 Scale = 138%

1:48 to 1:32 Scale = 150%

1:48 to 1:16 Scale = 300%

1:35 to 1:32 Scale = 109%

1:35 to 1:16 Scale = 218%

Rolls-Royce
Armored Car

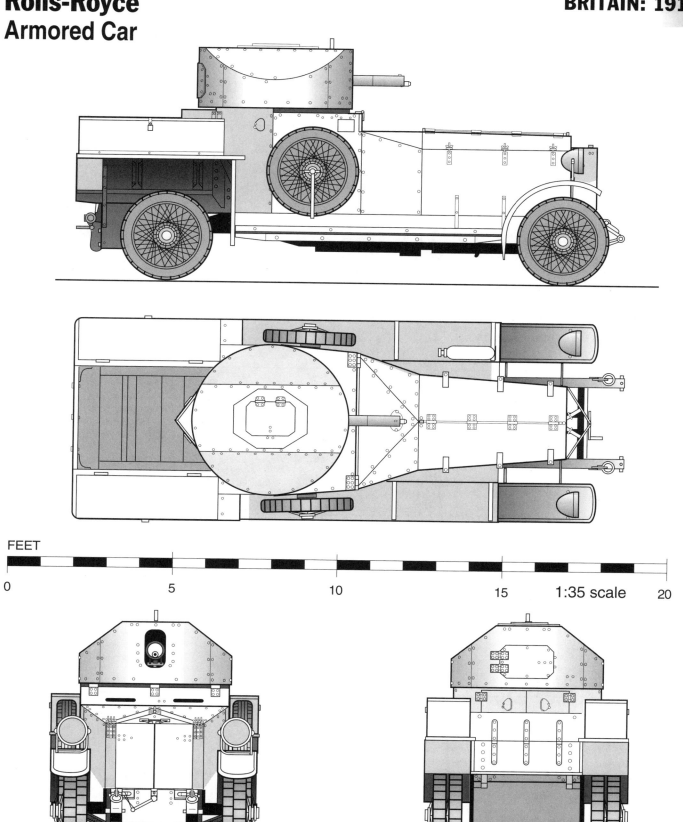

FEET

0   5   10   15   1:35 scale   20

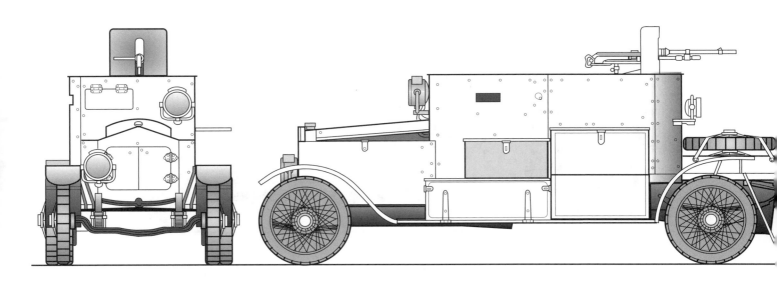

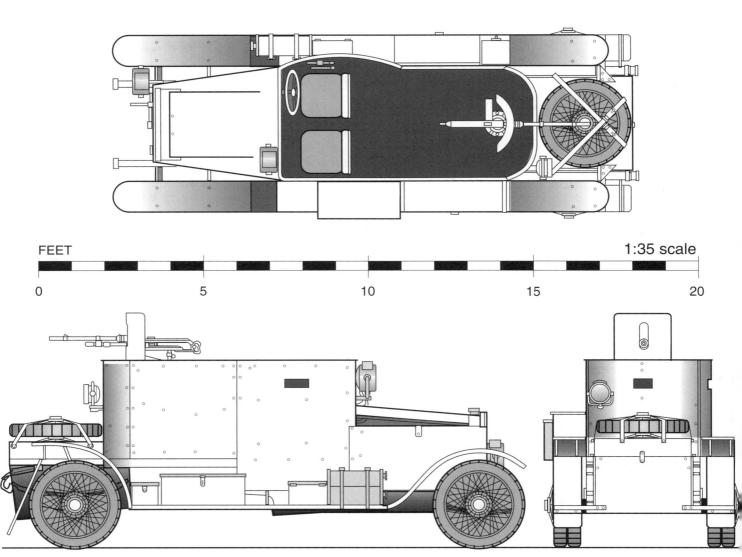

FEET   1:35 scale

0   5   10   15   20

Lanchester
Armored Car

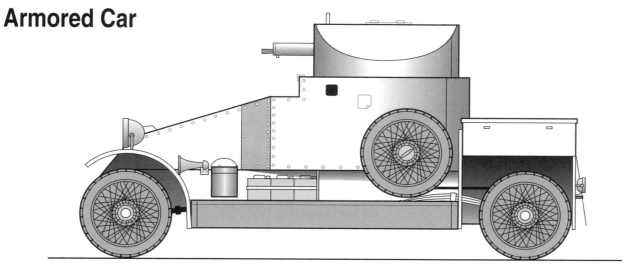

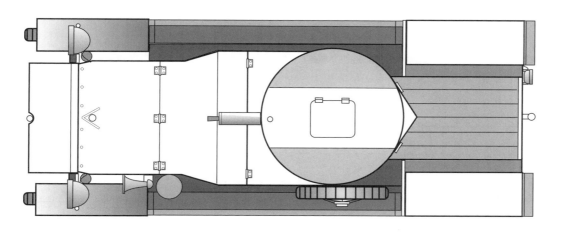

FEET   1:35 scale

0   5   10   15   20

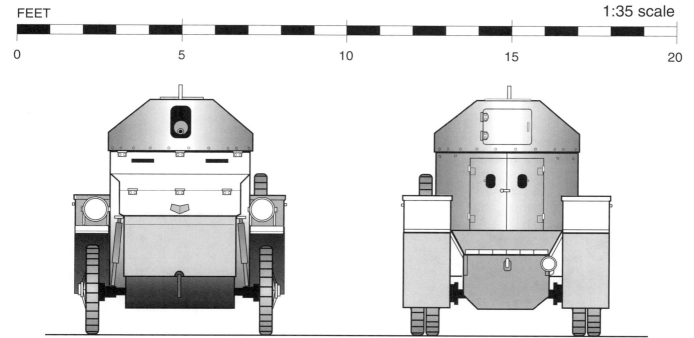

Little Willie
Early British Test Vehicle
Completed by December 1915

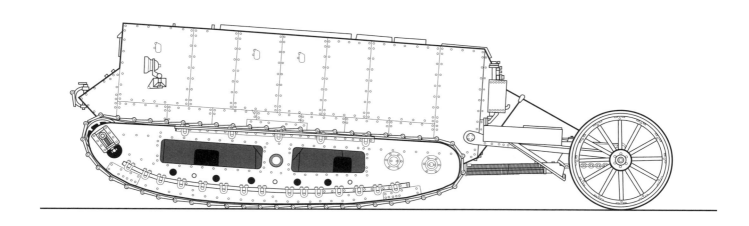

FEET

0   5   10   15   20

1:48 scale

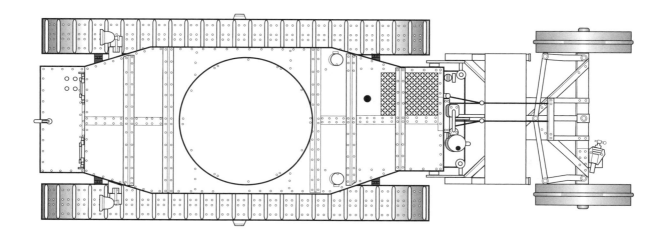

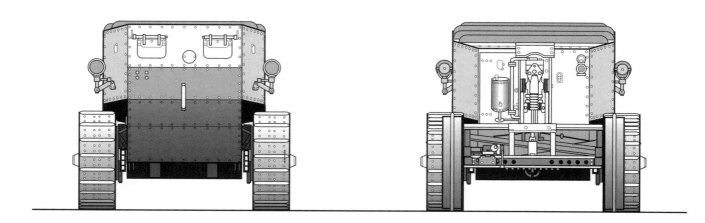

White
Armored Car

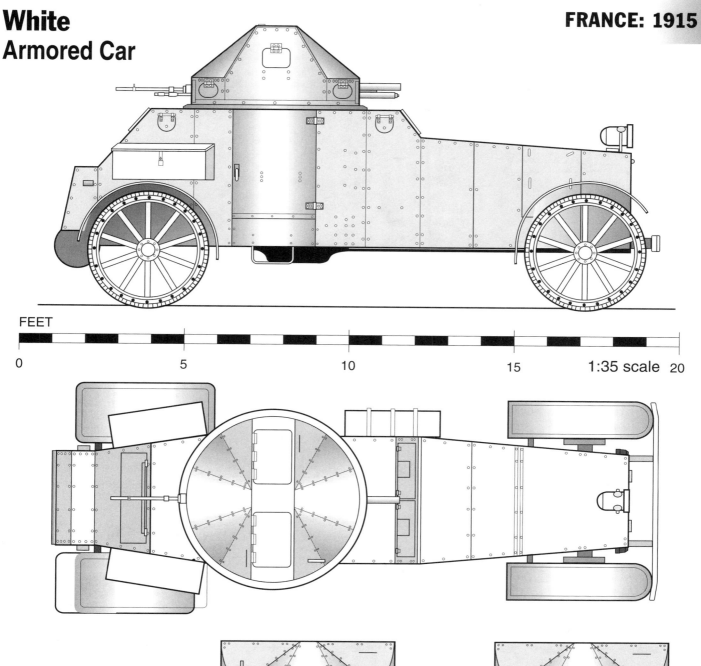

FEET

0   5   10   15   1:35 scale   20

During World War I about 20 armored cars known as Auto-mitrailleuse White were built on the White truck chassis supplied by the USA. Later in 1918 an additional 230 with righthand drive were built and soldiered on right into the 1940s, much like the British Rolls-Royce armored cars. The turret mounted a 37mm cannon in the front and a Hotch-kiss MG in the rear.

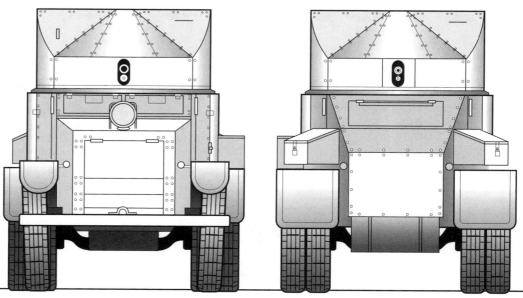

Mark I Tank (Male)

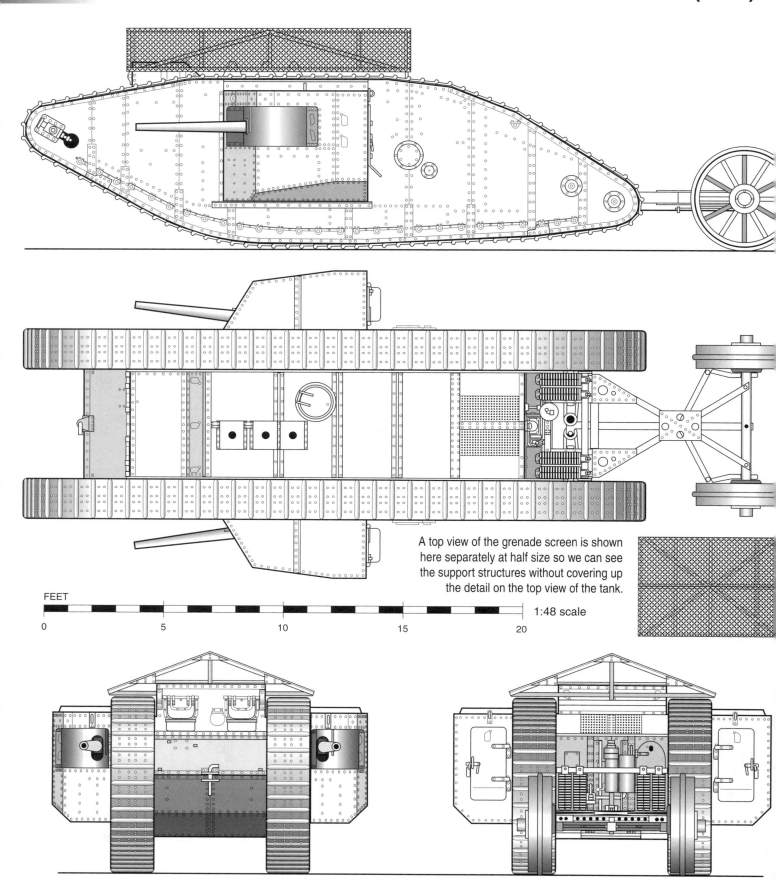

A top view of the grenade screen is shown here separately at half size so we can see the support structures without covering up the detail on the top view of the tank.

FEET

0   5   10   15   20

1:48 scale

Mark IV Tank (Female)

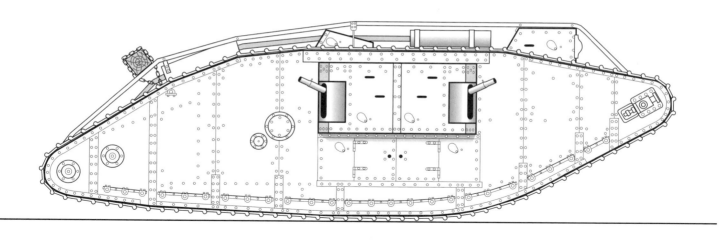

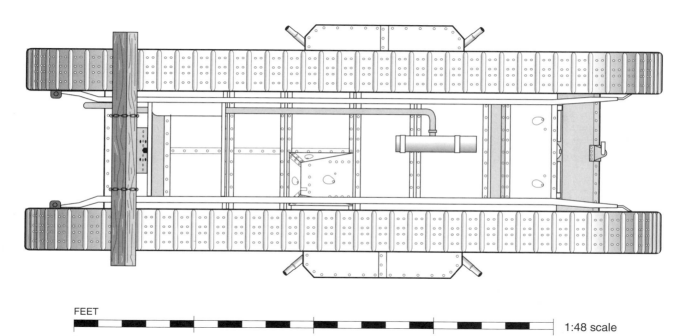

FEET

0   5   10   15   20

1:48 scale

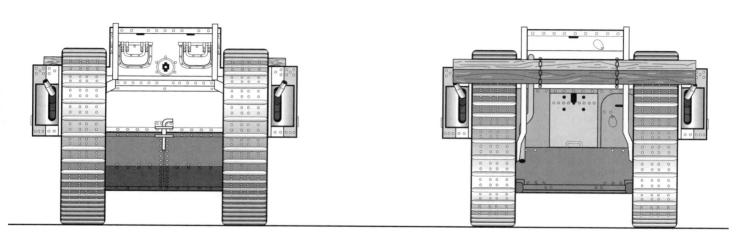

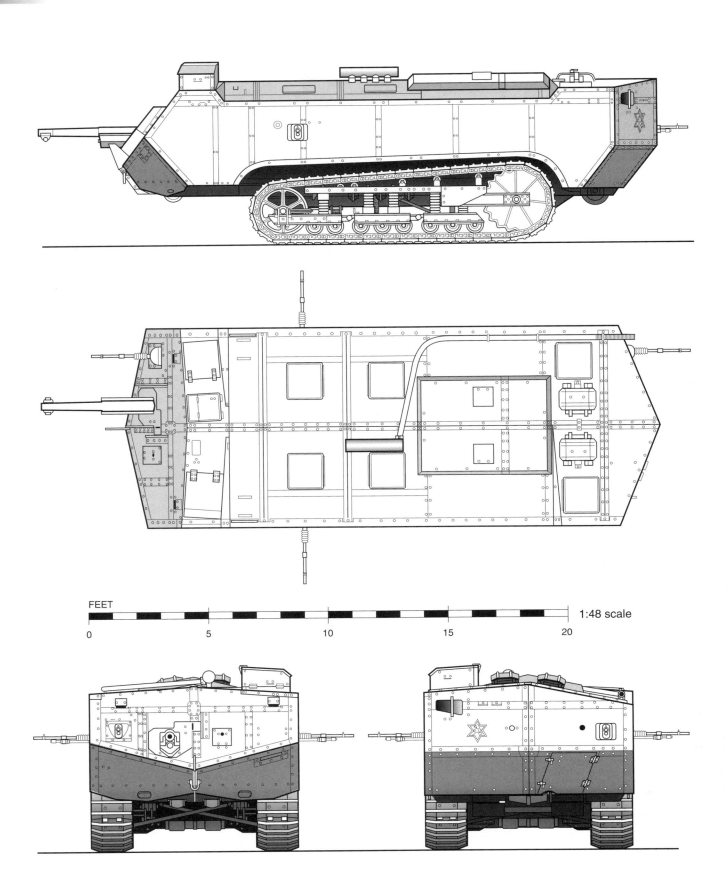

FEET

1:48 scale

0   5   10   15   20

Char Schneider CA 1

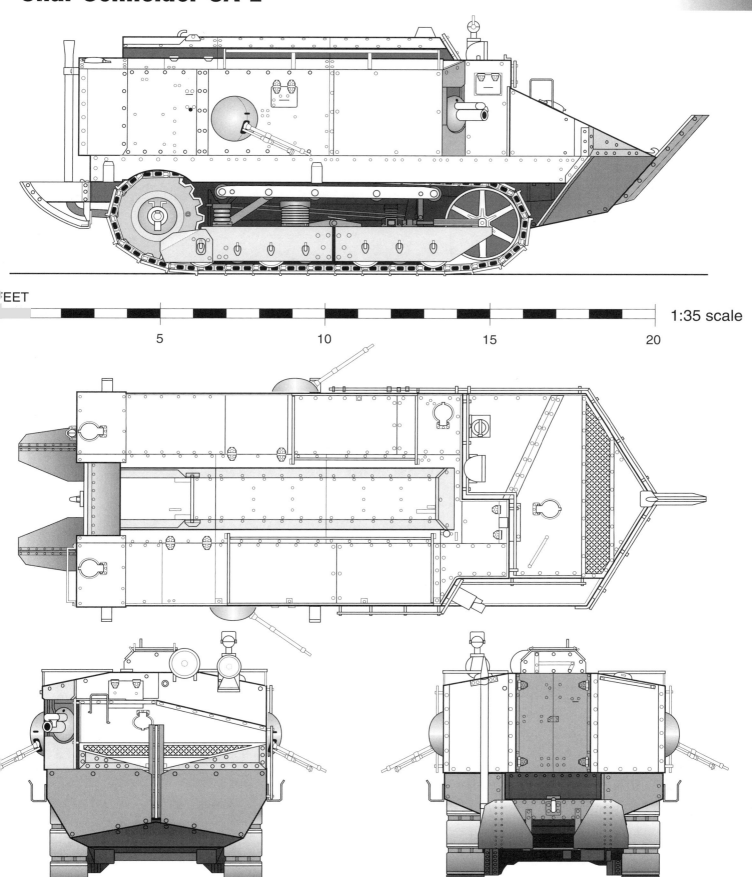

FEET

1:35 scale

5   10   15   20

Benz-Mgebrov Armored Car

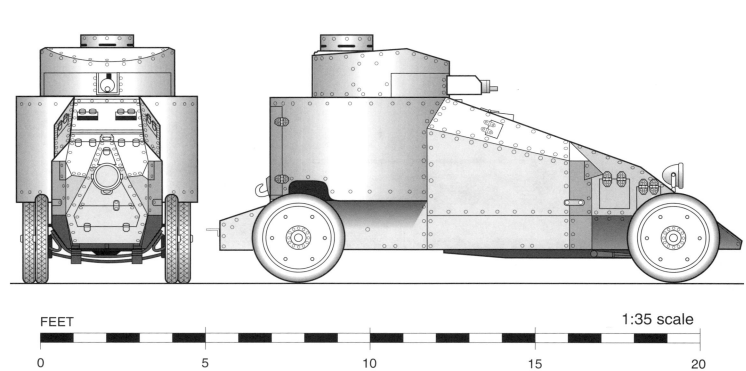

FEET   1:35 scale

0   5   10   15   20

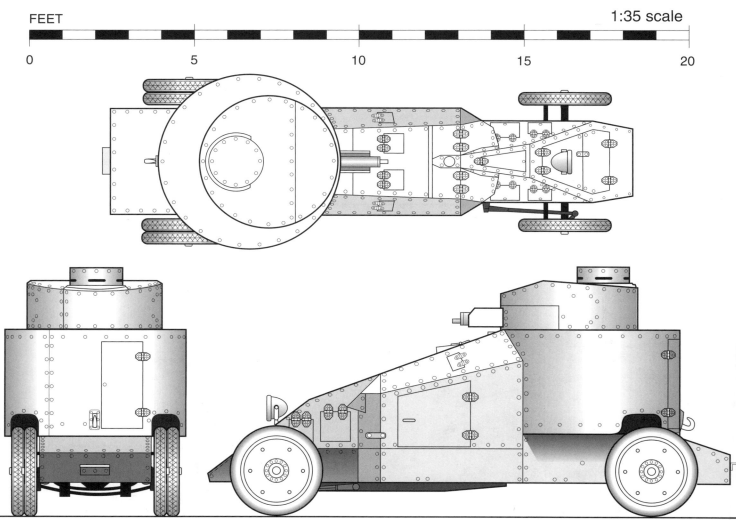

Garford-Putilov Armored Car

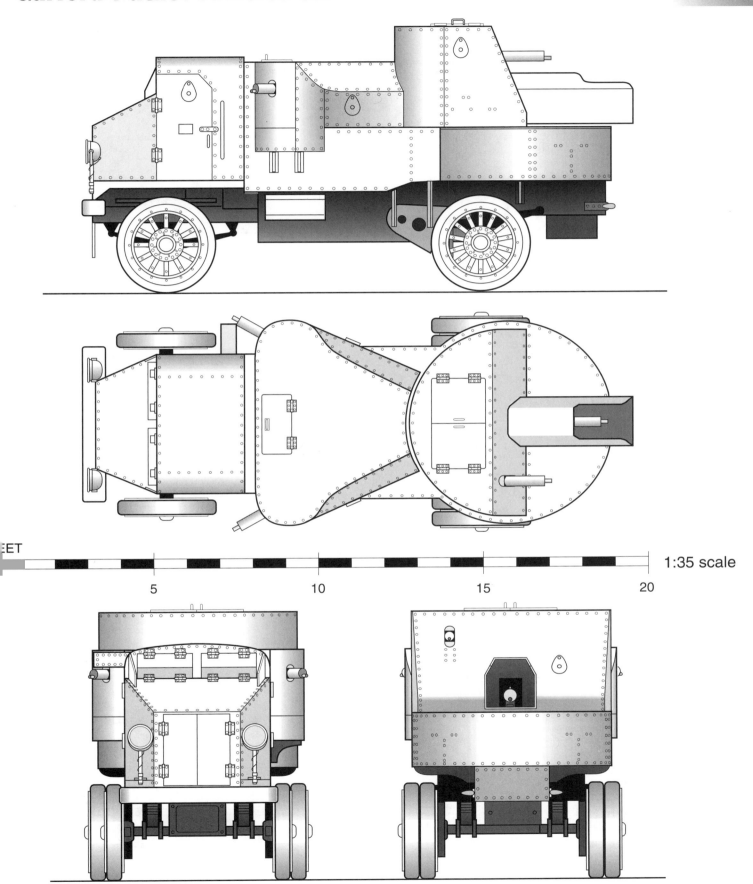

FEET

1:35 scale

5   10   15   20

Austin-Putilov
Armored Car

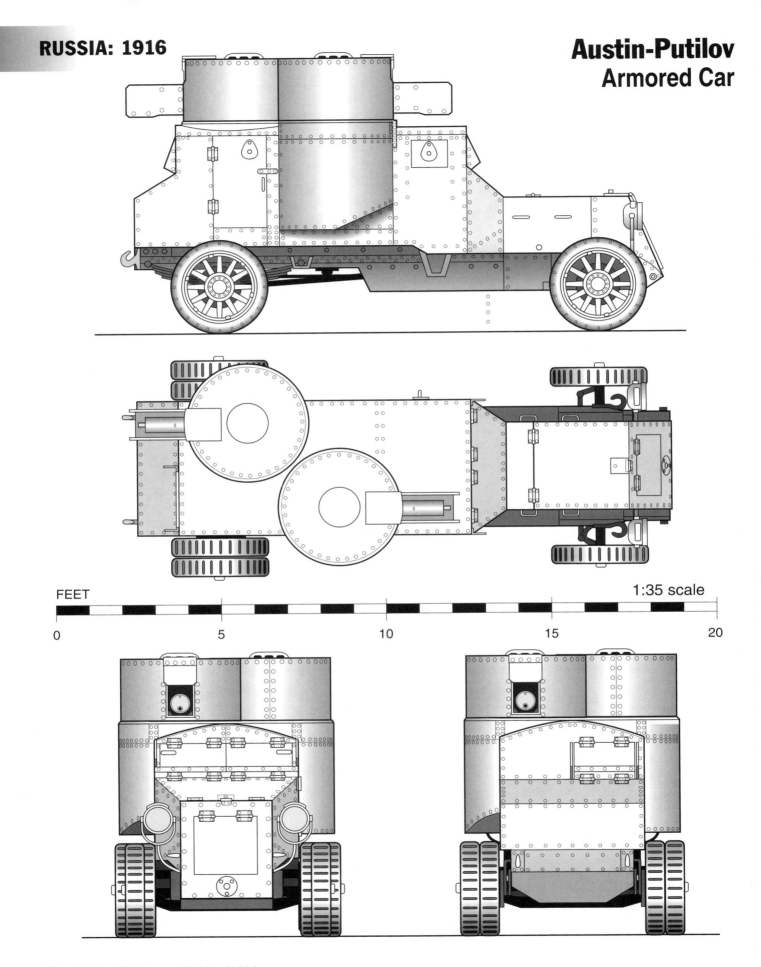

FEET

1:35 scale

0   5   10   15   20

Mark IV Tank (Male)
with 6-pdr guns

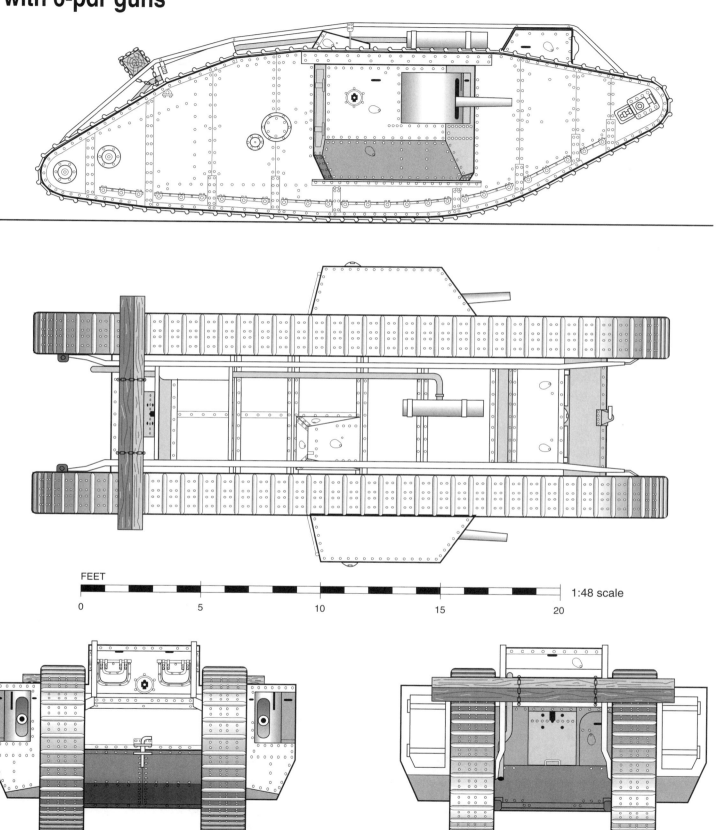

FEET

1:48 scale

0   5   10   15   20

Austin-Kegresse
Armored Car

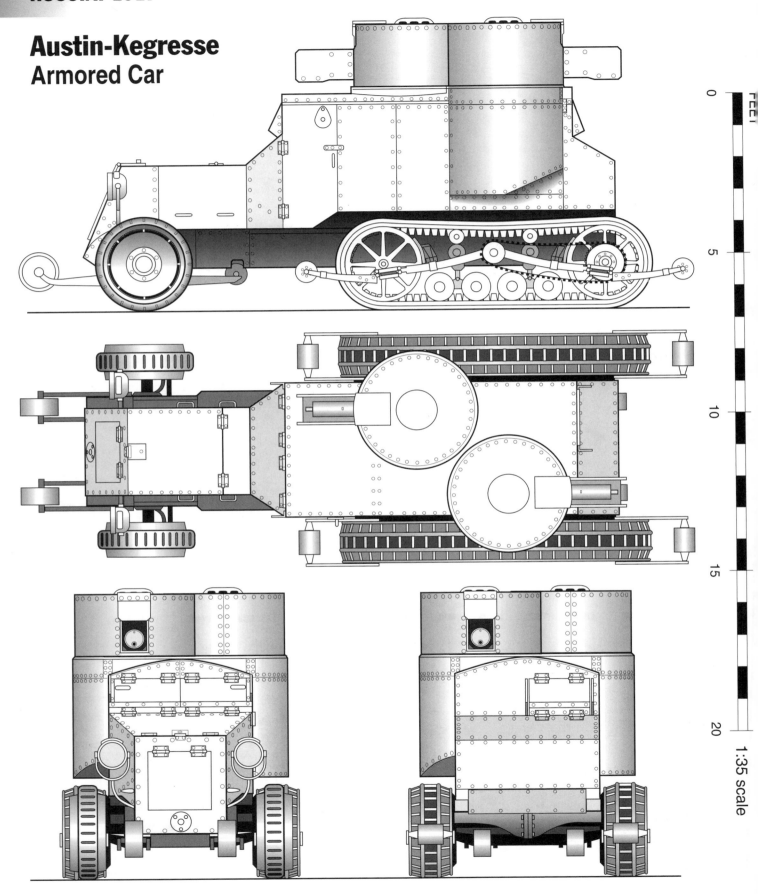

Mark IV
Tadpole Tank
(Male)

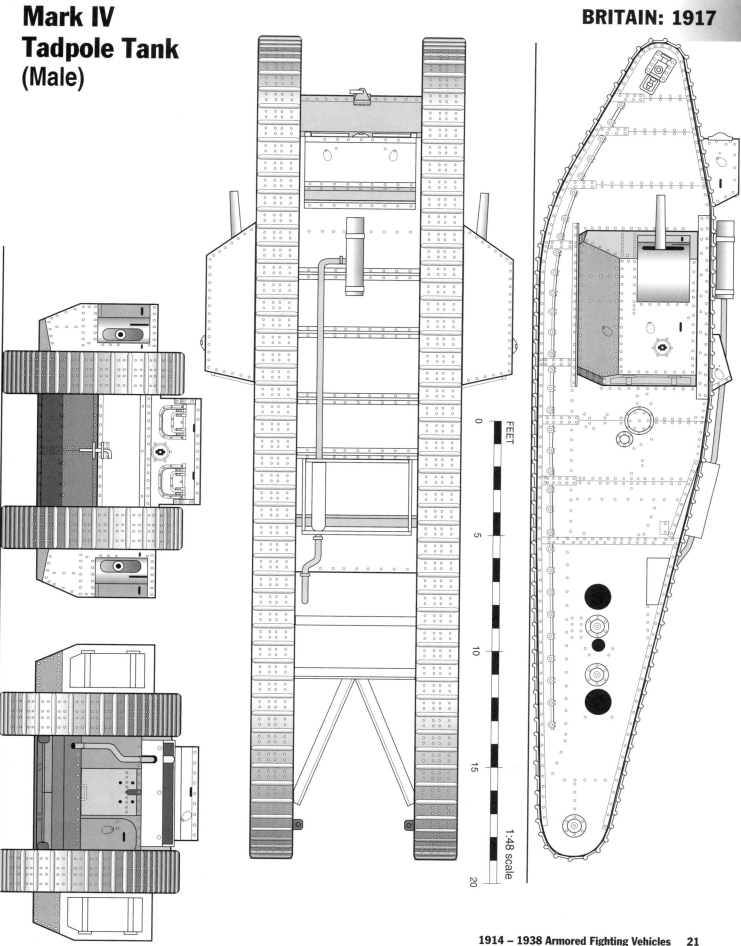

FEET

0

5

10

15

20

1:48 scale

Armored Autocar
Canadian Machine Gun Carrier
Drawings courtesy of Chris Johnson

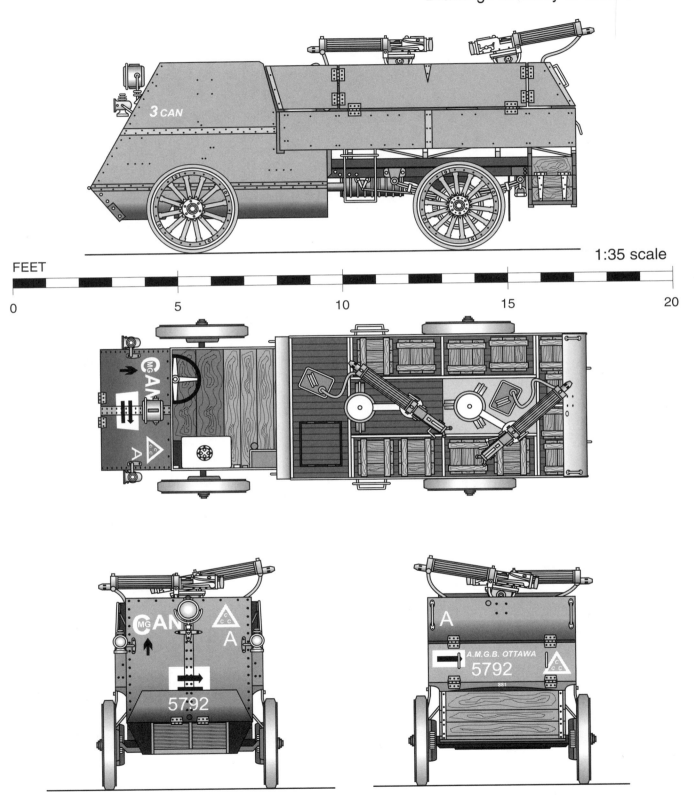

1:35 scale

FEET

0   5   10   15   20

Lancia 1ZM Armored Car
(Abm Ansaldo)

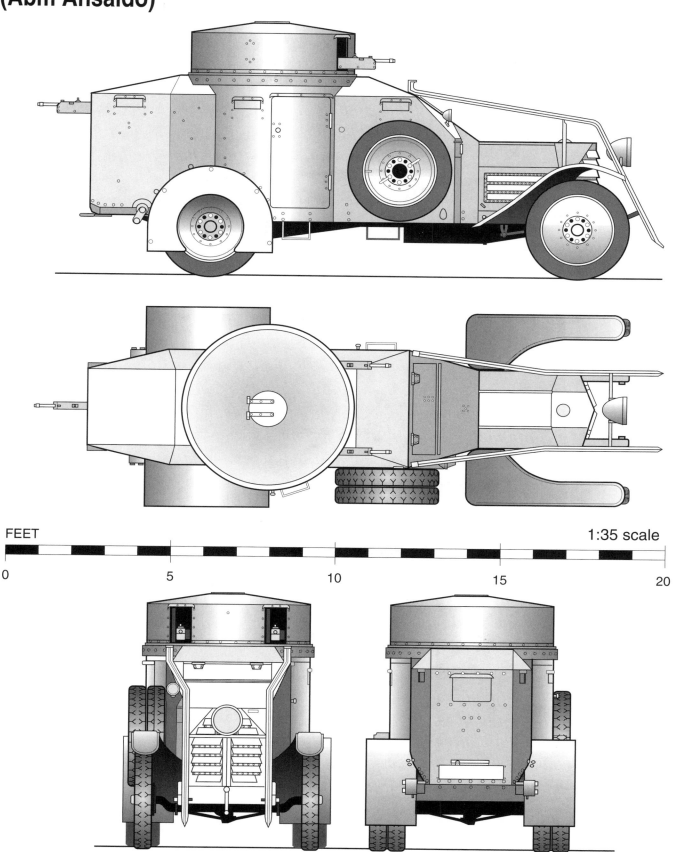

FEET

1:35 scale

0   5   10   15   20

Medium Mark A Whippet Tank

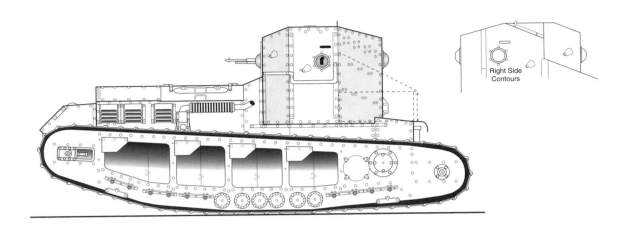

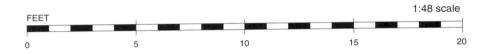

FEET

1:48 scale

0   5   10   15   20

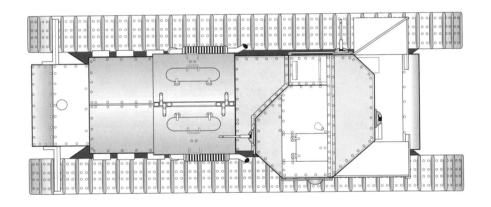

Right Side
Contours

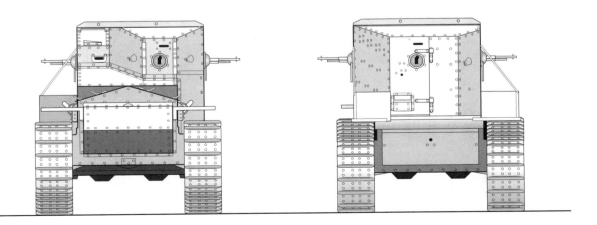

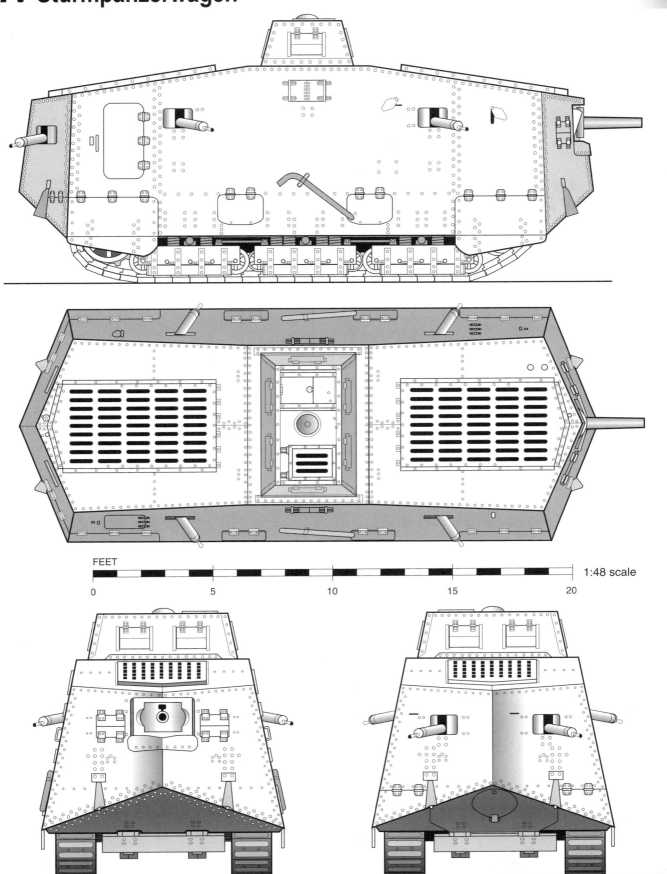

FEET

0   5   10   15   20

1:48 scale

Char-mitrailleuse **Renault FT-17**

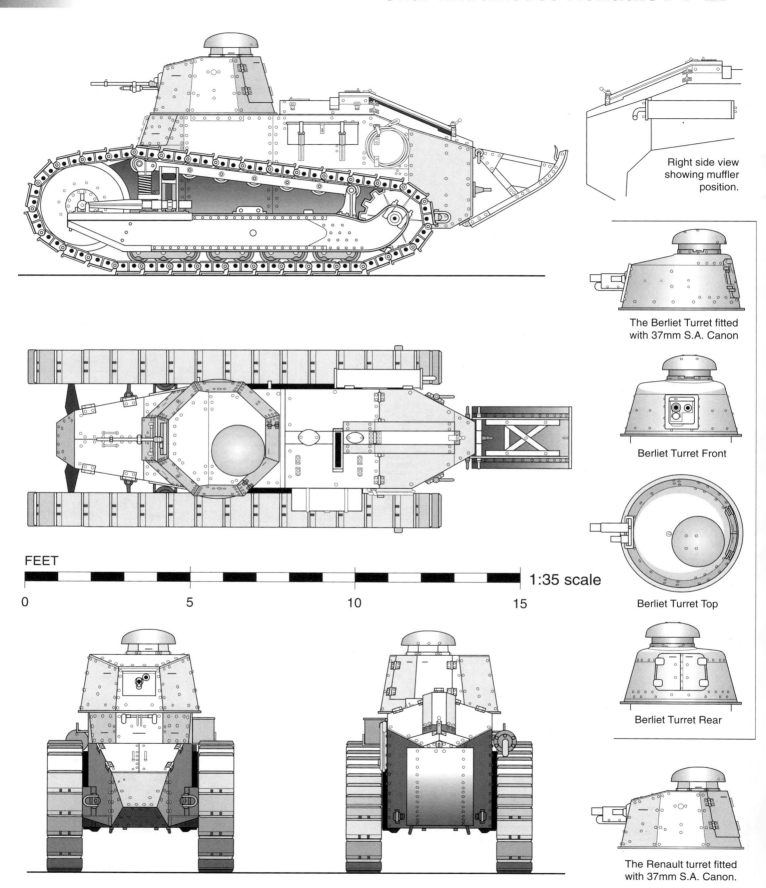

Right side view showing muffler position.

The Berliet Turret fitted with 37mm S.A. Canon

Berliet Turret Front

Berliet Turret Top

Berliet Turret Rear

The Renault turret fitted with 37mm S.A. Canon.

FEET

0   5   10   15

1:35 scale

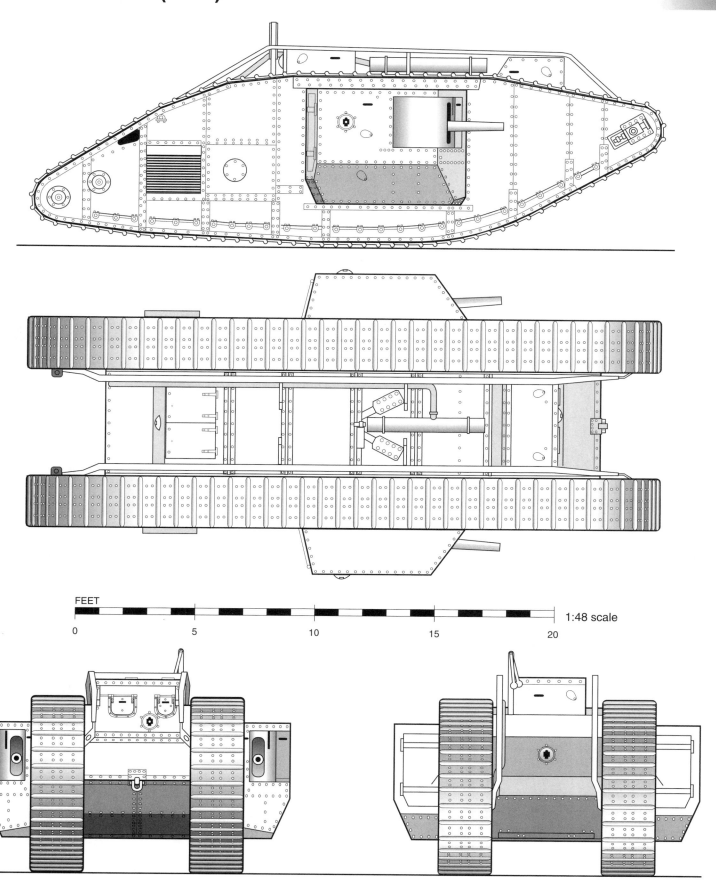

FEET

1:48 scale

0   5   10   15   20

White-Laffly Armored Car
(AMD Laffly 50 AM)

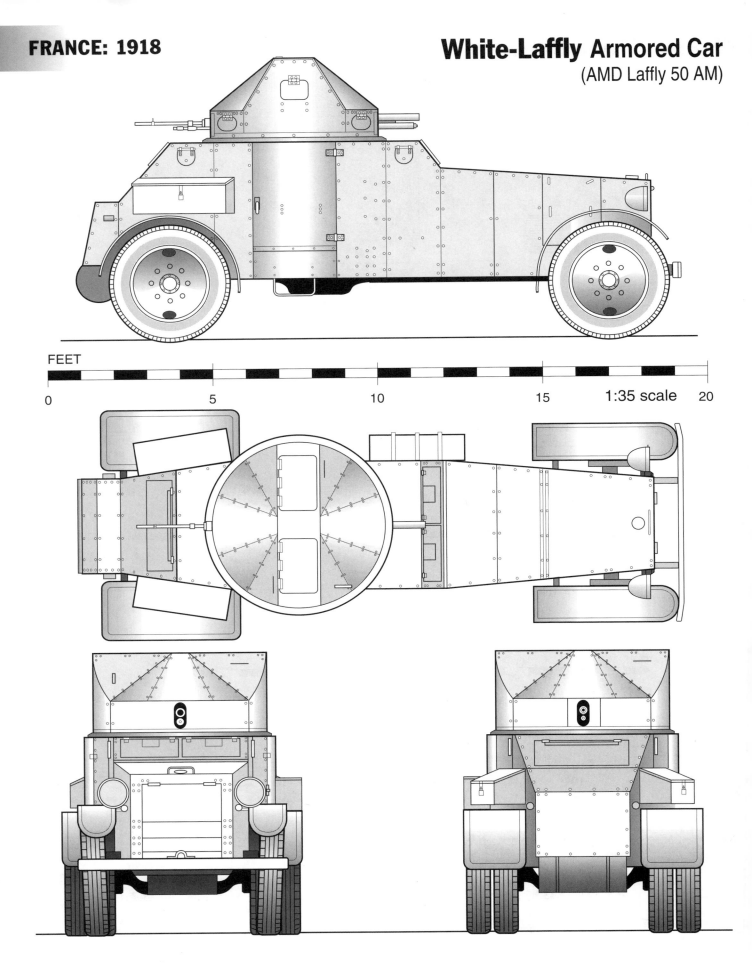

FEET

0   5   10   15   1:35 scale   20

Ford 3-Ton Tank
3-Ton Special Tractor M1918

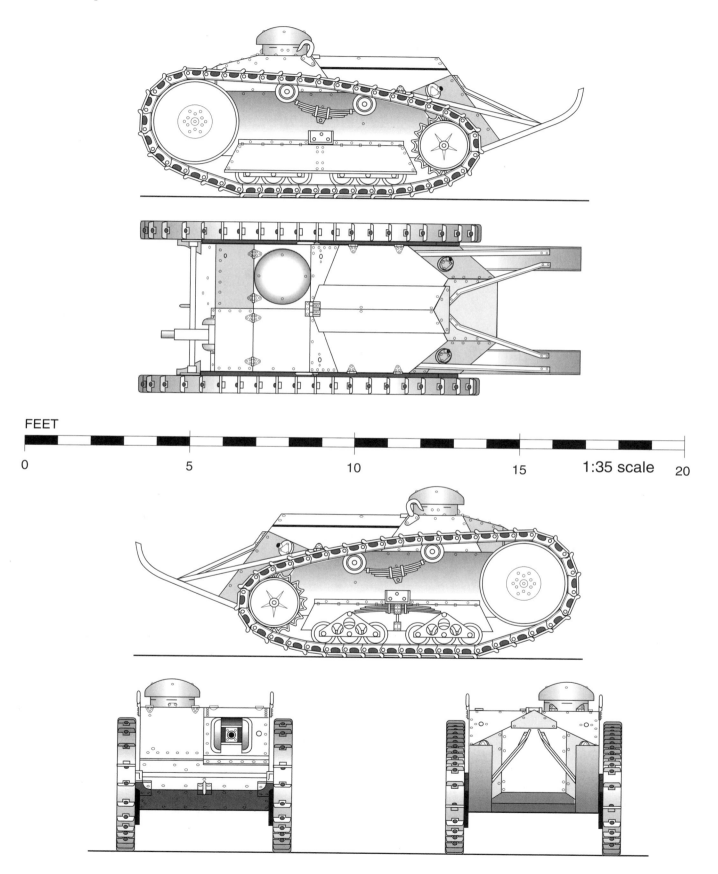

FEET

0   5   10   15   1:35 scale   20

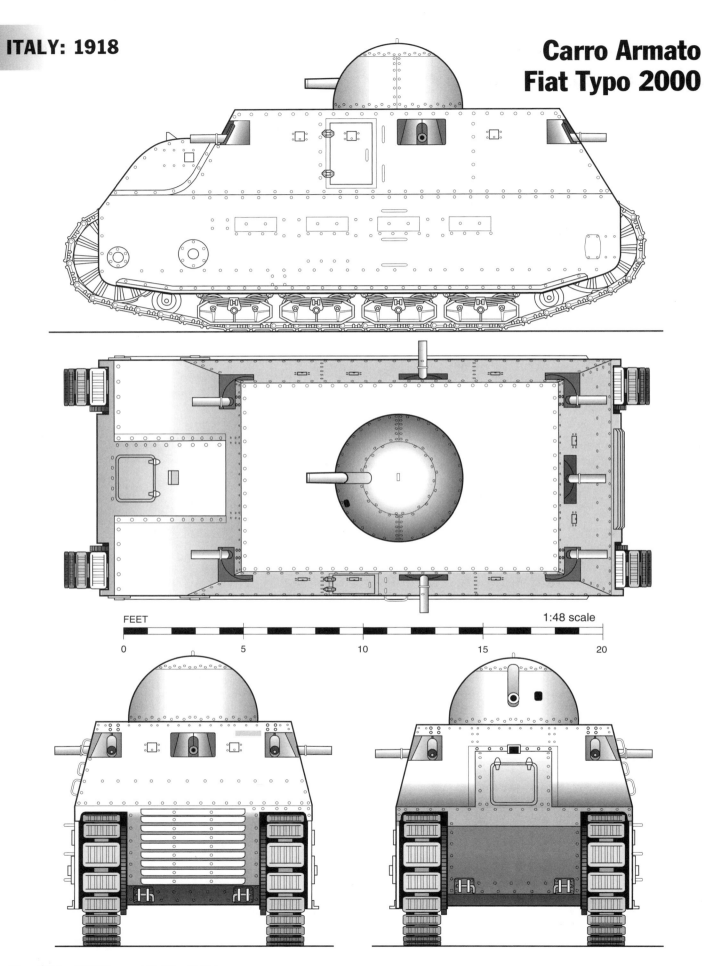

FEET

0   5   10   15   20

1:48 scale

M1917 6-Ton Tank
Light Tank

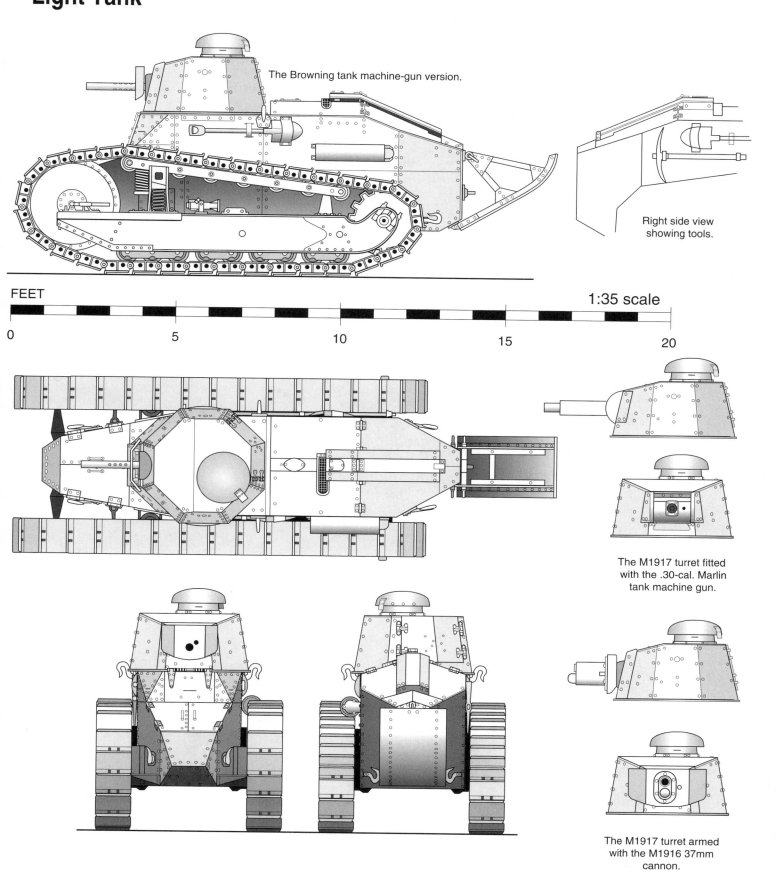

The Browning tank machine-gun version.

Right side view showing tools.

FEET

1:35 scale

0   5   10   15   20

The M1917 turret fitted with the .30-cal. Marlin tank machine gun.

The M1917 turret armed with the M1916 37mm cannon.

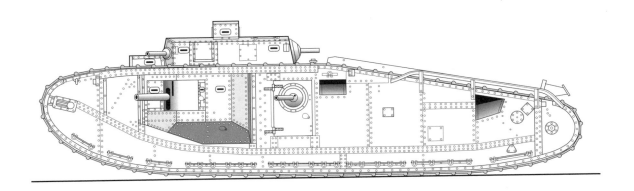

FEET

1:72 scale

0   5   10   15   20

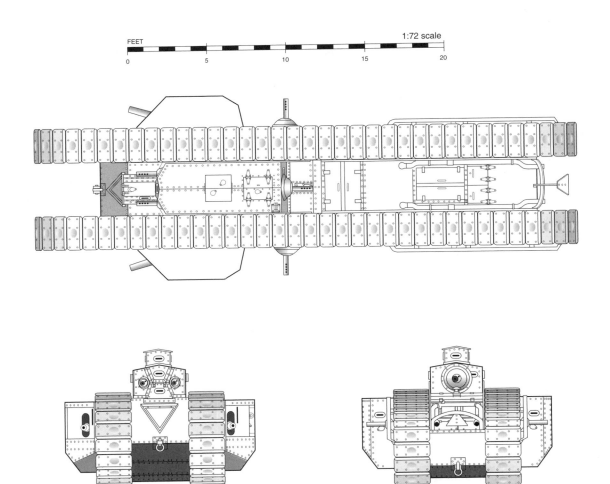

Carro armato Fiat 3000 Mod. 21
(L.5/21)

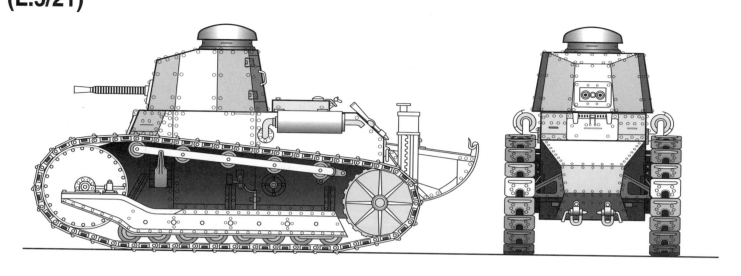

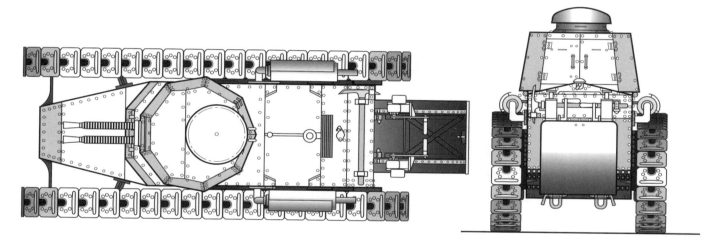

FEET

0   5   10   15   20

1:35 scale

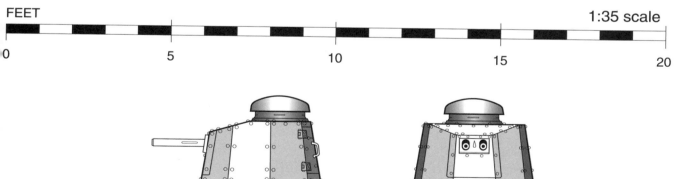

The optional turret design fitted with twin S.I.A. machine guns.

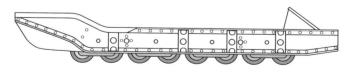

Shown here is the longer suspension beam also found on
later Mod. 21s, more like the one used on the Mod. 30.

Rolls-Royce Armored Car
RAF Type A, 1920 Pattern Mark I

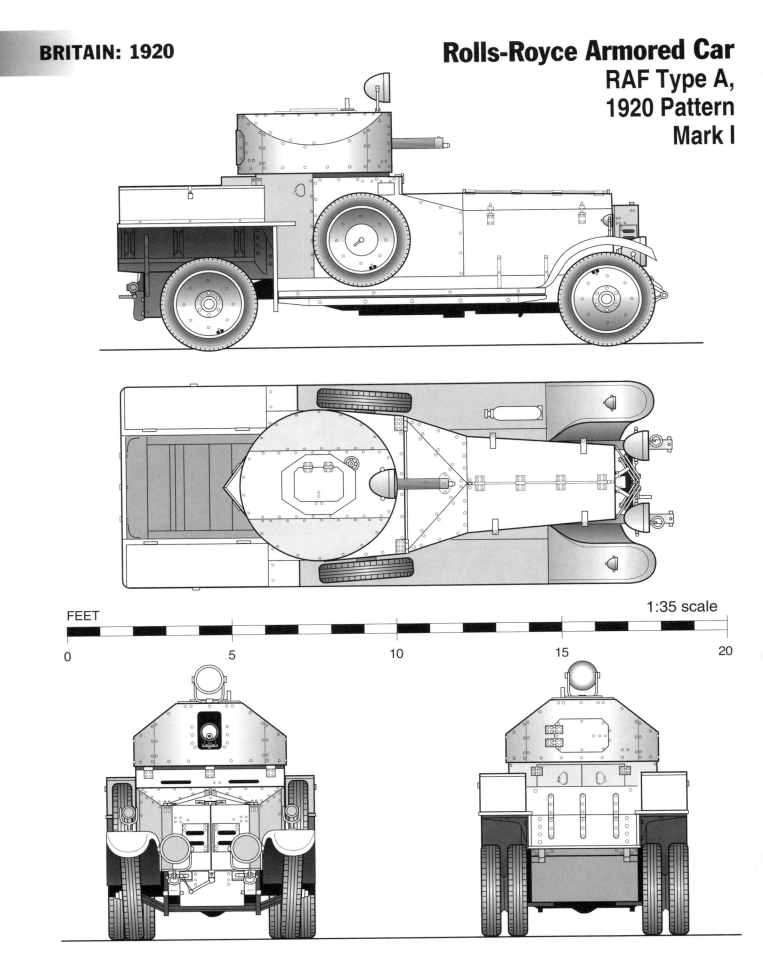

FEET

1:35 scale

0   5   10   15   20

T1E2 Light Tank
Fitted with high-velocity semi-automatic 37mm gun and .30-cal MG

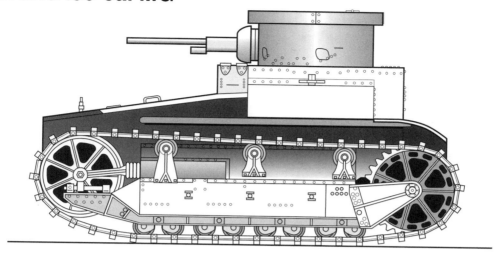

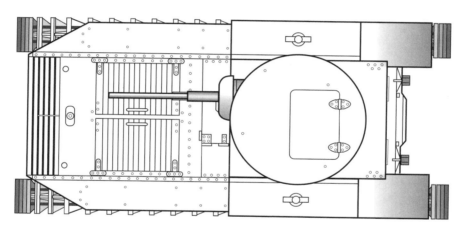

FEET

1:35 scale

0   5   10   15   20

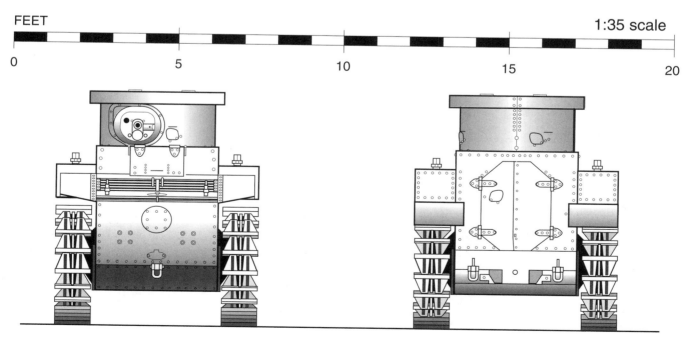

Rolls-Royce Armored Car
1924 Pattern,
Mark I

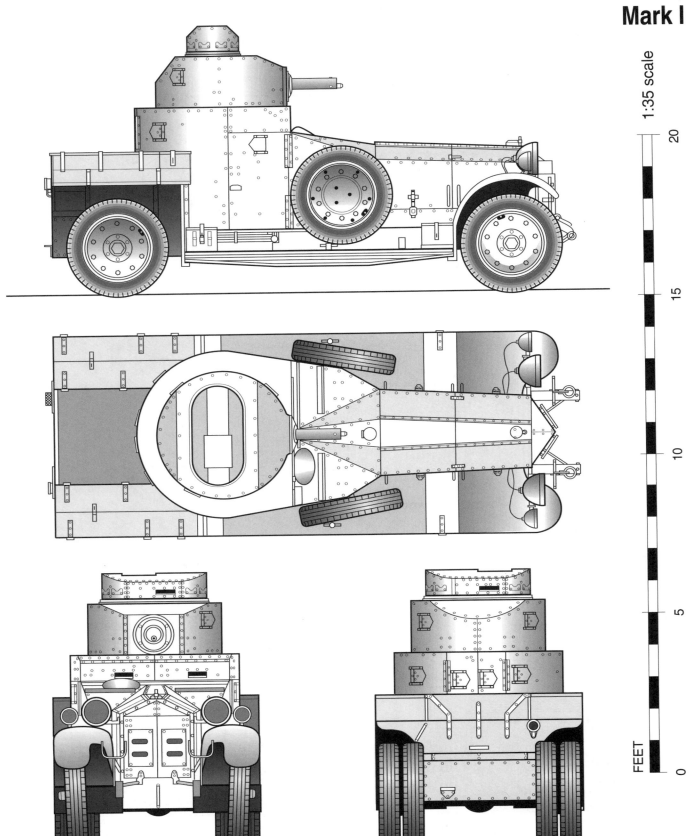

1:35 scale

BA-27 Armored Car
On the AMO-F-15 truck chassis and later on the Ford AA chassis.

FEET

0   5   10   15   20

1:35 scale

Skoda PA-III, OA vz. 27
Armored Car

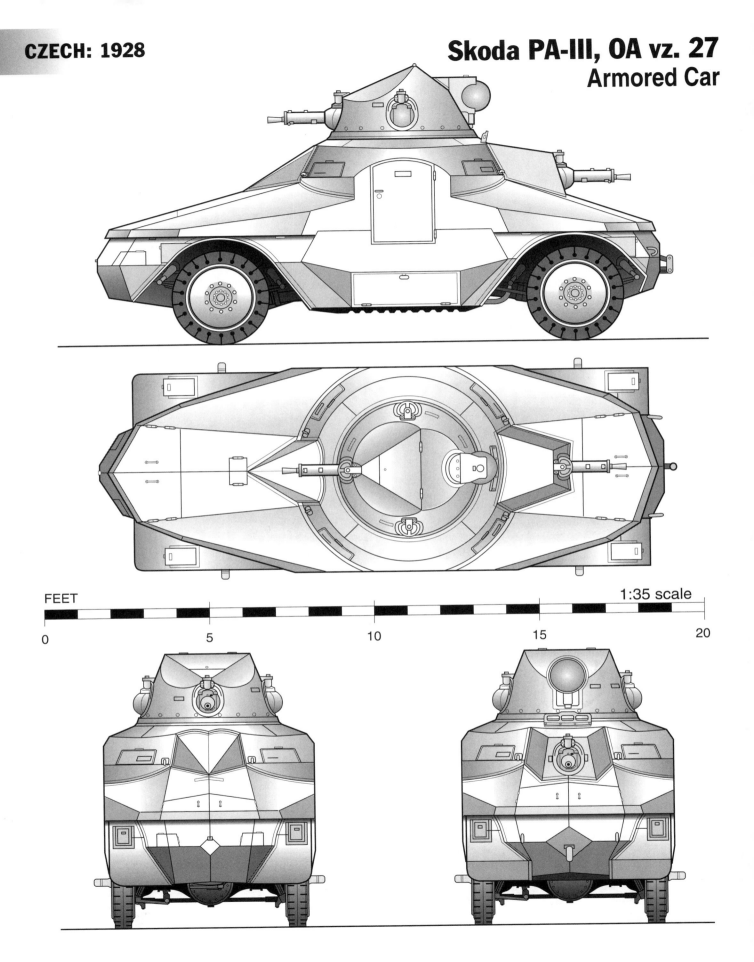

FEET

1:35 scale

0   5   10   15   20

T7 Franklin
Armored Car

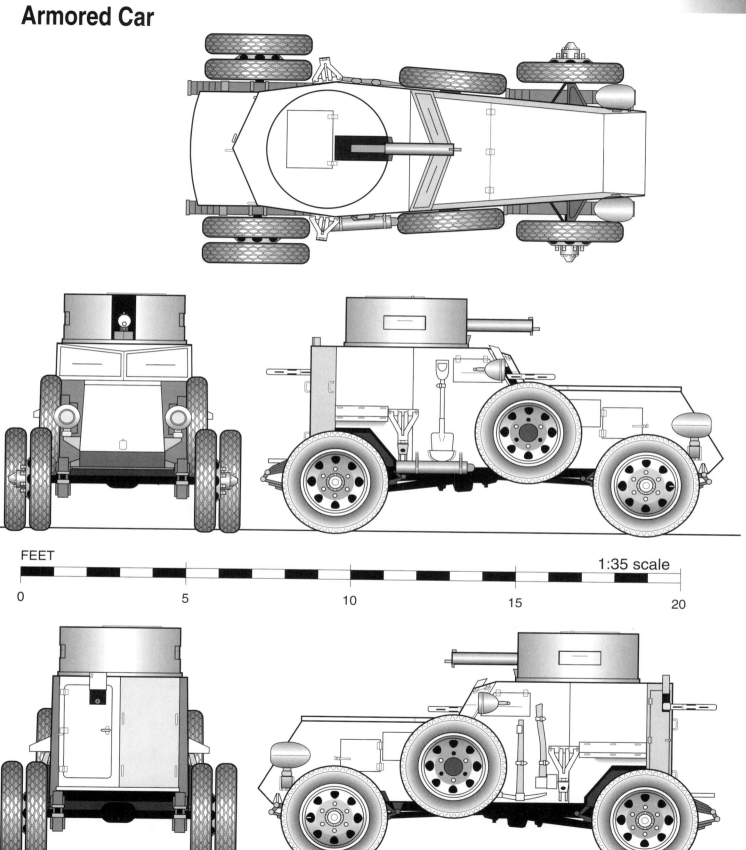

FEET

1:35 scale

0   5   10   15   20

FEET

0   5   10   15   20

1:72 Scale

FAI-M Armored Car
on the GAZ-M-1 chassis

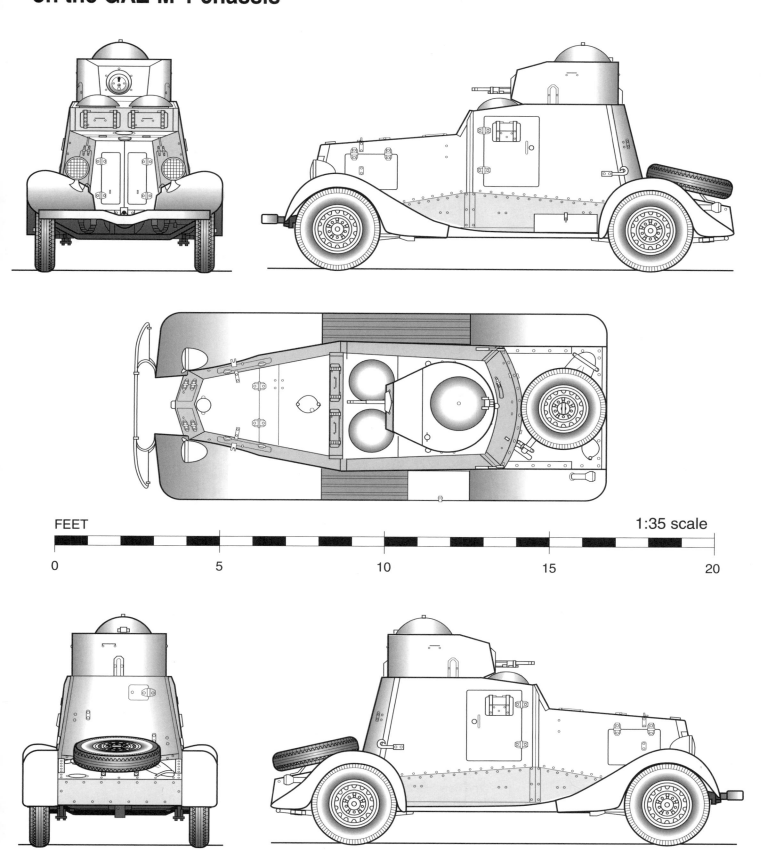

FEET   1:35 scale

0   5   10   15   20

Carro Armato Fiat 3000, Model 30
(L.5/30)

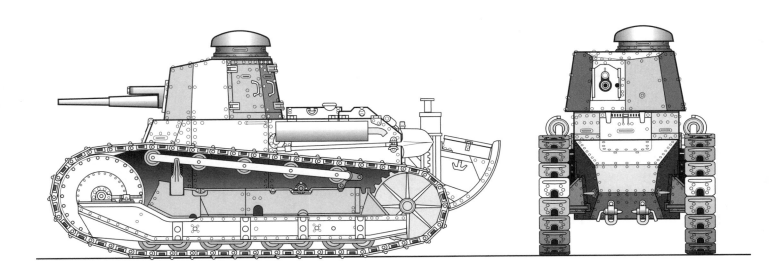

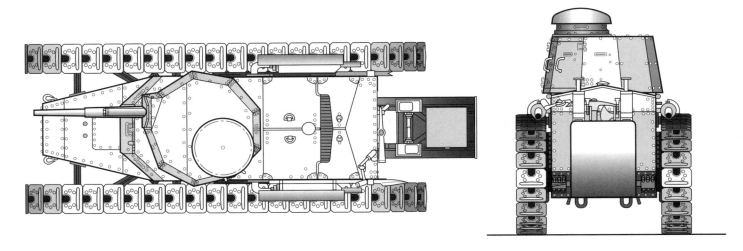

FEET

1:35 scale

0   5   10   15   20

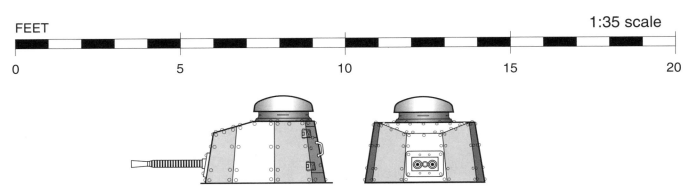

The new Fiat 3000 Mod. 30 chassis was also
fitted with the Fiat twin 6.5 machine gun armed
turrets from the earlier Mod. 21.

AMC Schneider P16 (M29)
Citroën-Kégresse Half-Tracked
Armored Car

FEET

1:35 scale

0   5   10   15   20

37133

37133

Lanchester Mark II
Armored Car

1:35 scale

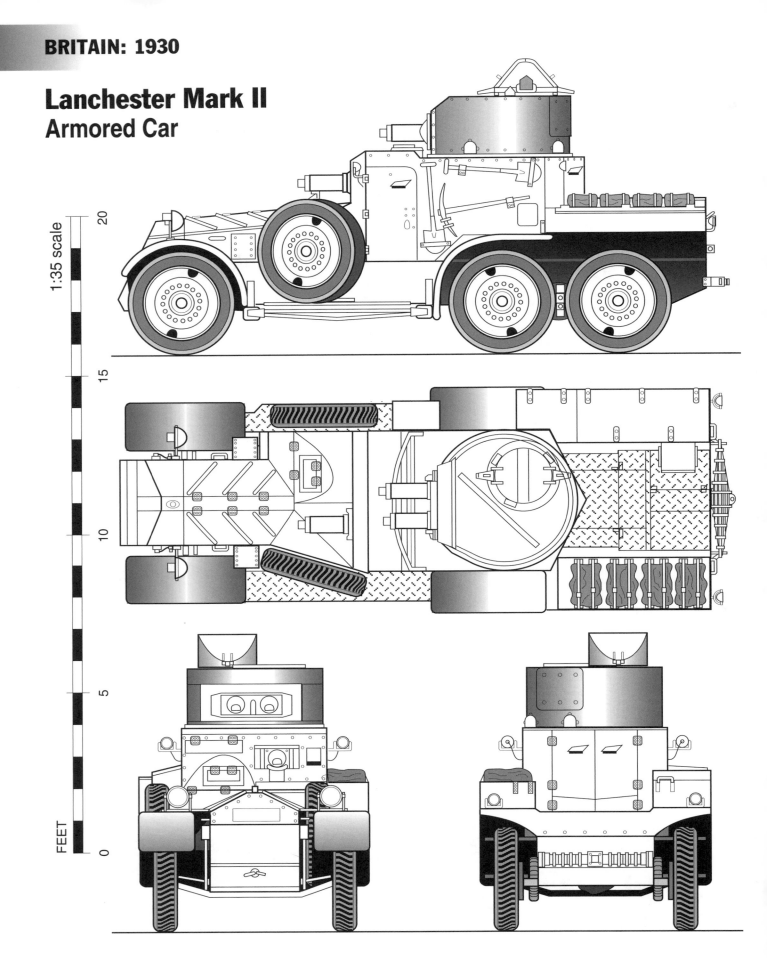

20

15

10

5

FEET

0

Char Renault D1 Tank
(with ST2 turret)

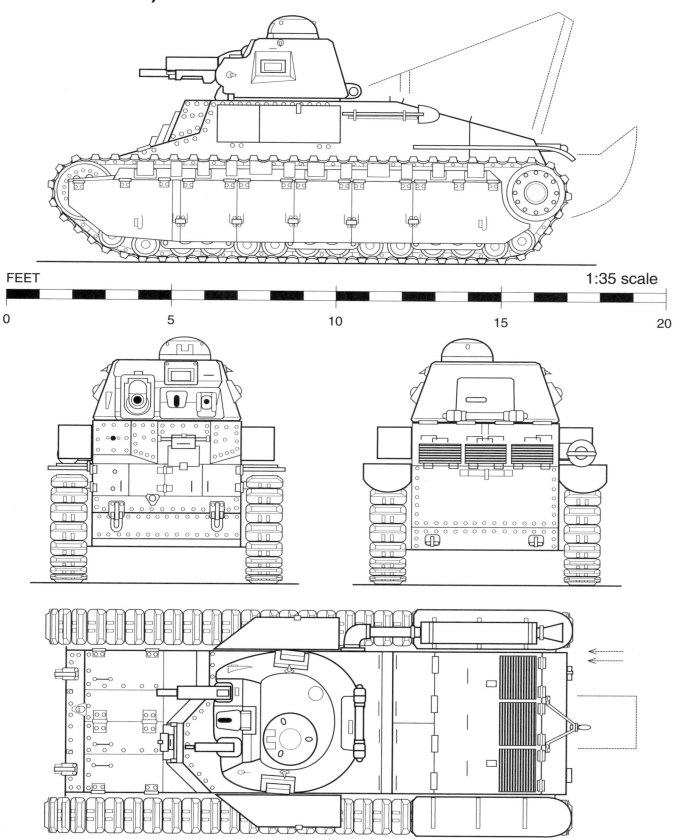

FEET

1:35 scale

0   5   10   15   20

BA-27M Armored Car
on the Ford-Timken chassis

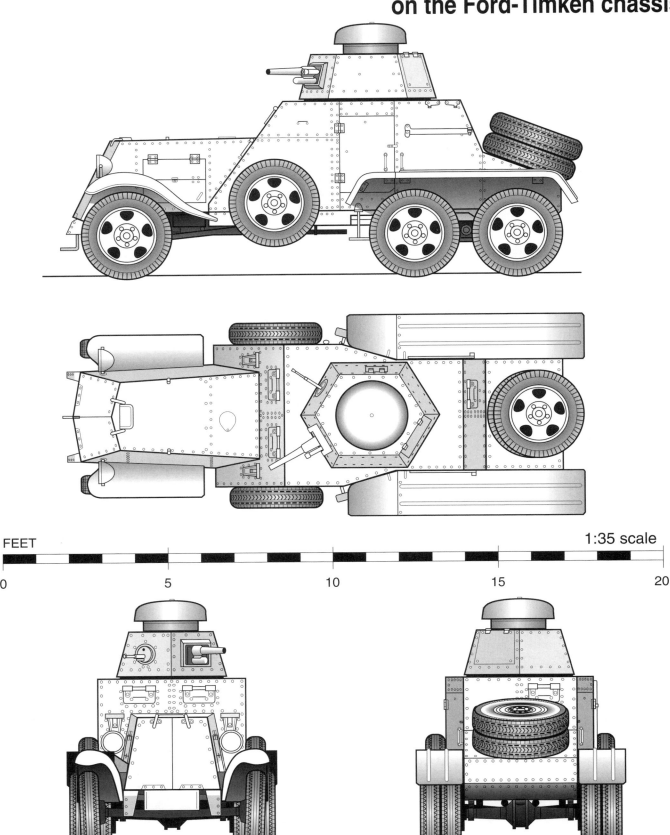

FEET

1:35 scale

0   5   10   15   20

T-26 Model 1931 Light Tank

with T-26TU command tank aerial and 37mm gun turret inset

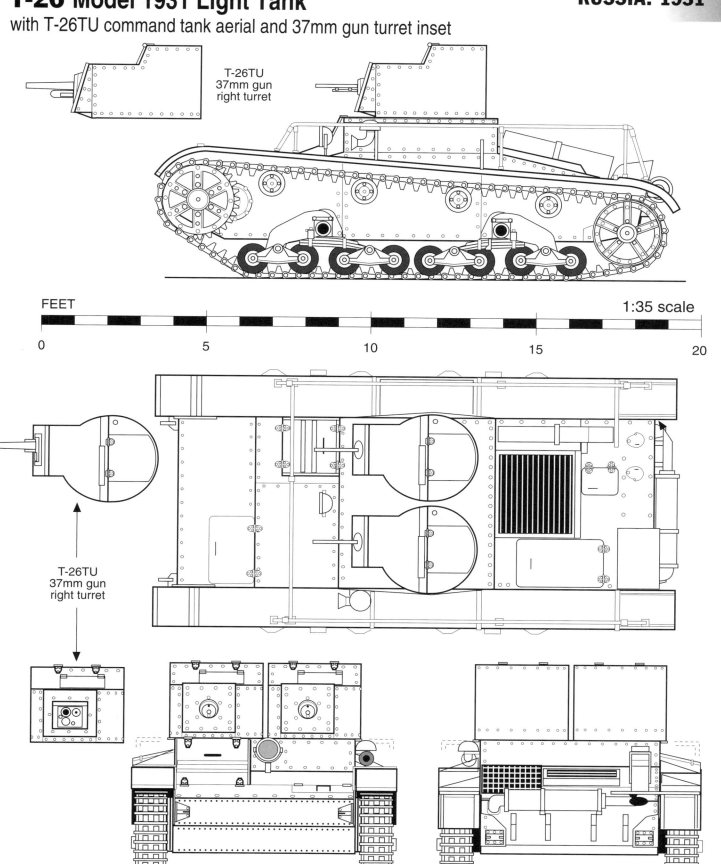

T-26TU
37mm gun
right turret

FEET   1:35 scale

0   5   10   15   20

T-26TU
37mm gun
right turret

Char Renault D2
with SA34 47mm gun

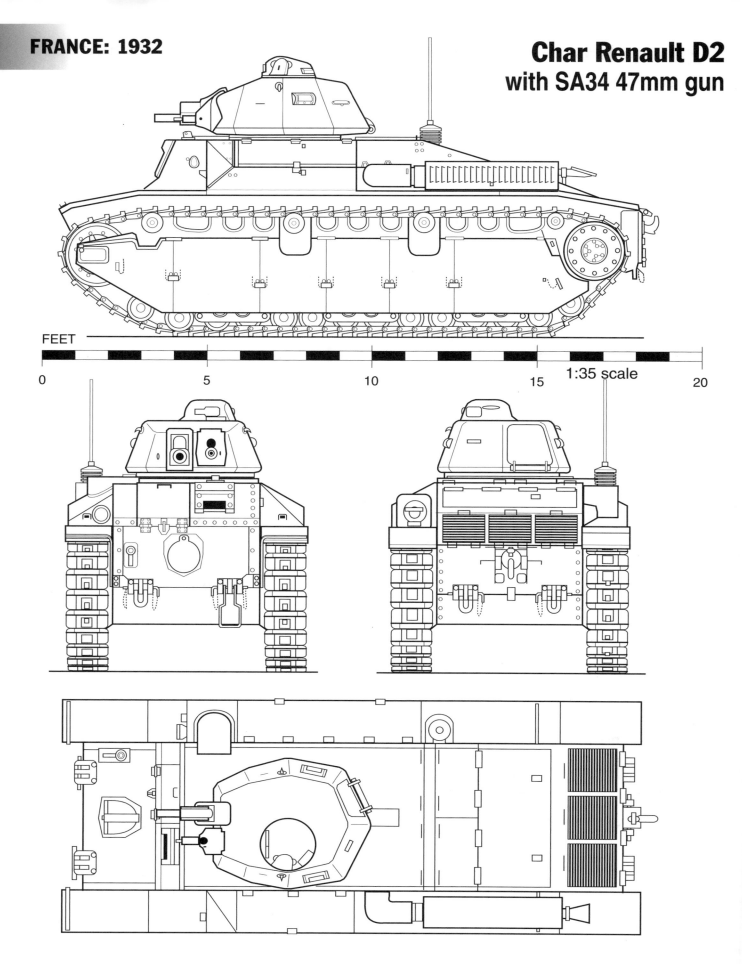

FEET

0   5   10   15   20

1:35 scale

TK-3 Light Recon Tankette
Standard TK-3 with 7.92mm Hotchkiss wz. 25 machine gun.

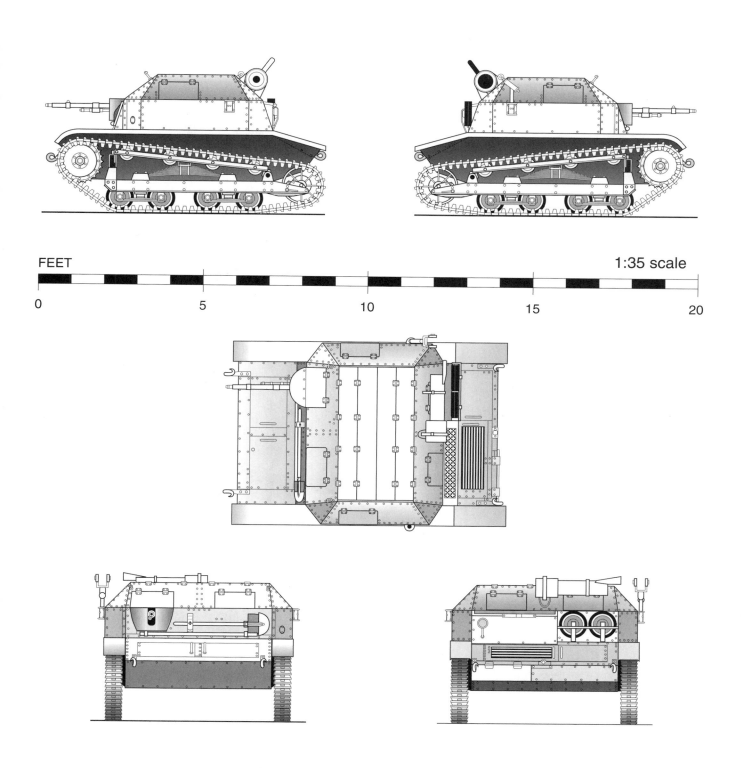

FEET

1:35 scale

0   5   10   15   20

Ursus wz. 29 Armored Car
Built on the chassis of the 1928 Ursus 2.5-ton truck.

1:35 scale

FEET

0   5   10   15   20

Gepanzerter Kraftwagen
(Sd.Kfz. 3)

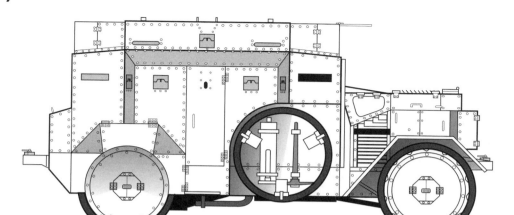

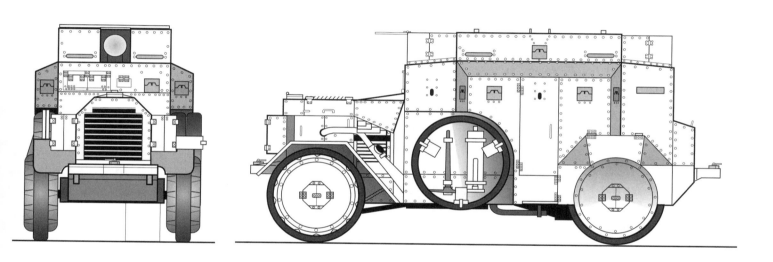

FEET   1:48 scale

0   5   10   15   20

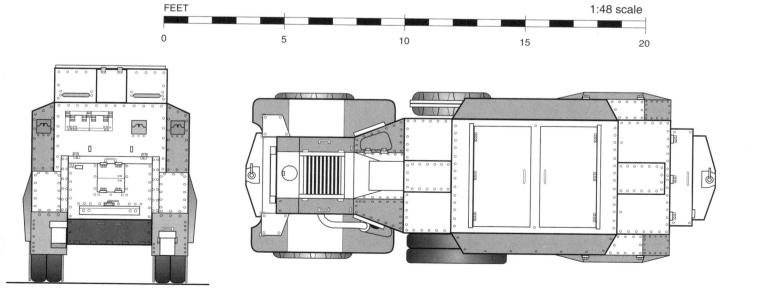

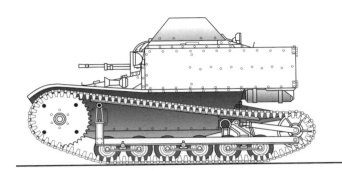
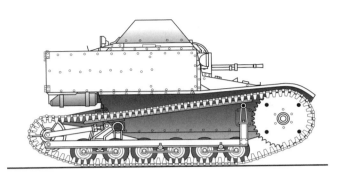

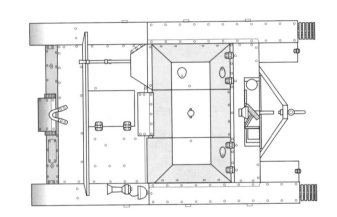

FEET
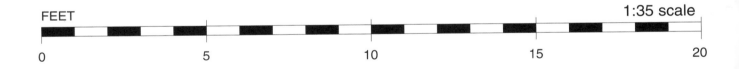

1:35 scale

0   5   10   15   20

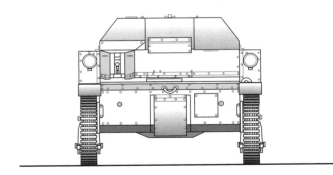
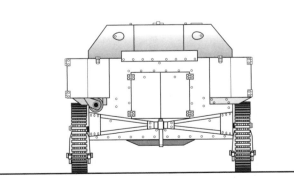

T-24 Medium Tank

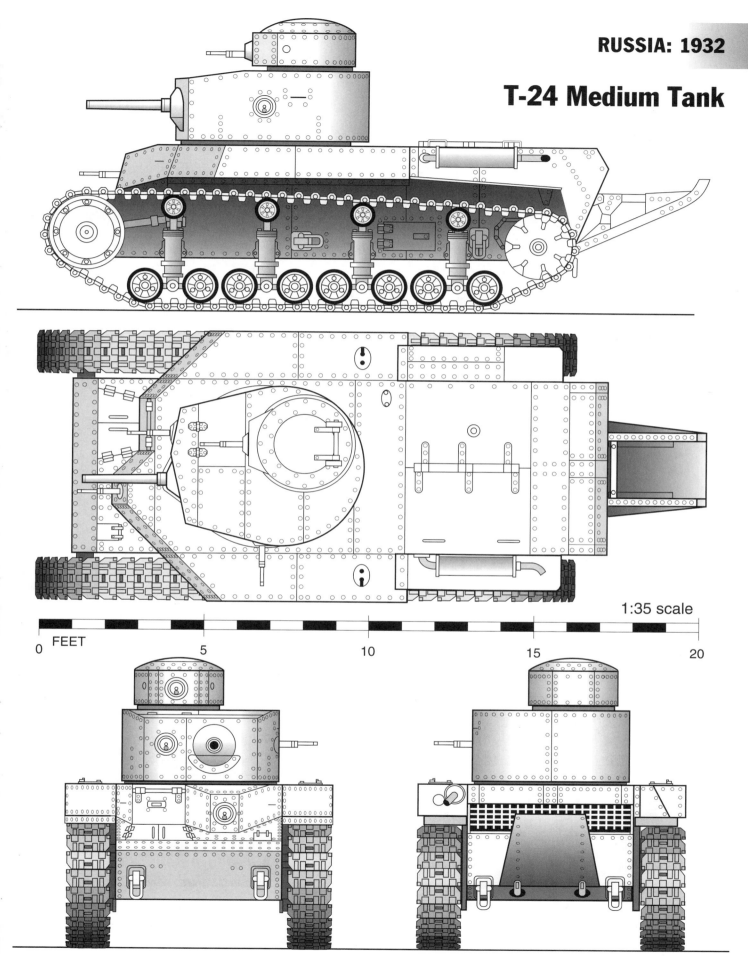

1:35 scale

FEET

0   5   10   15   20

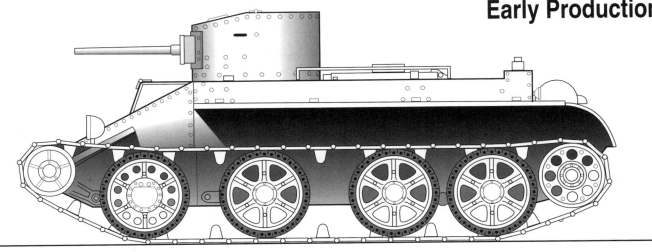

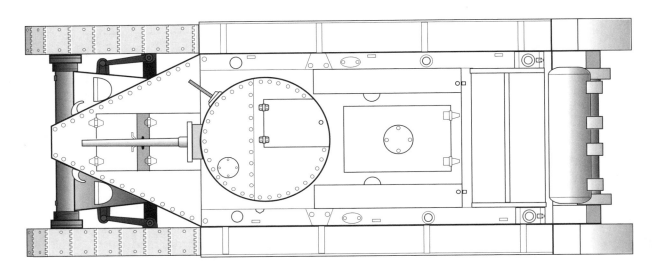

FEET

1:35 scale

0   5   10   15   20

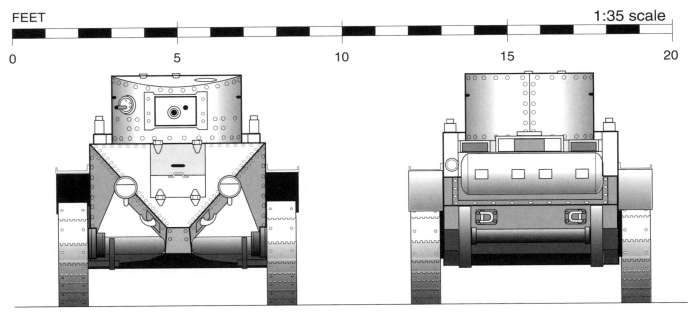

T3 Medium Tank
(Christie M.1931)

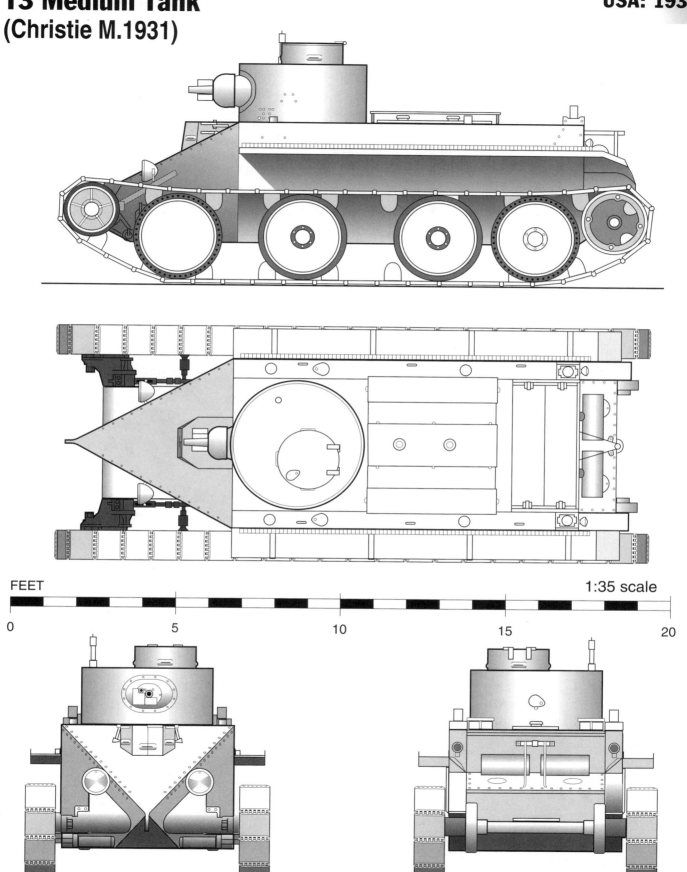

FEET

1:35 scale

0   5   10   15   20

Vickers-Armstrong
Mark III Medium Tank

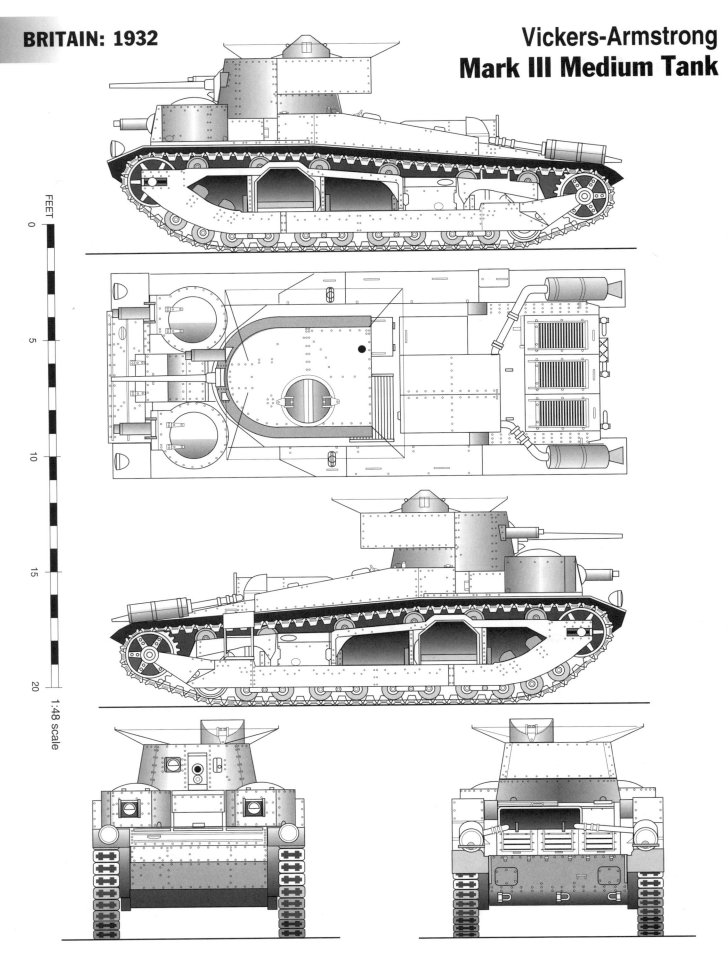

FEET

0

5

10

15

20

1:48 scale

Carro Veloce L3/33 Tankette
(C.V. L 3-33/II serie)
fitted with two 8mm Fiat model 14/35 MGs

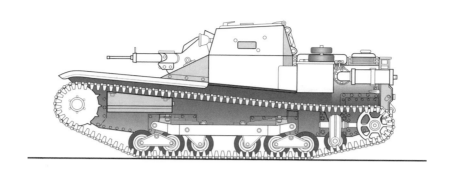

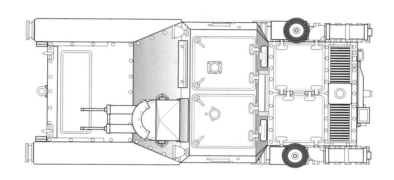

FEET   1:35 scale

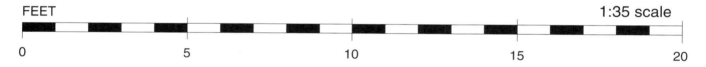

0   5   10   15   20

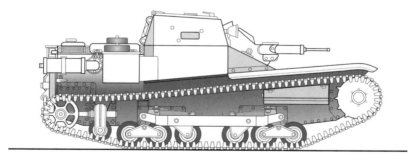

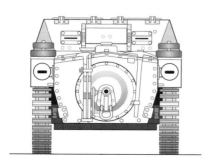

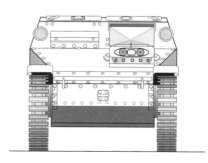

T-26 Model 1933 Light Tank

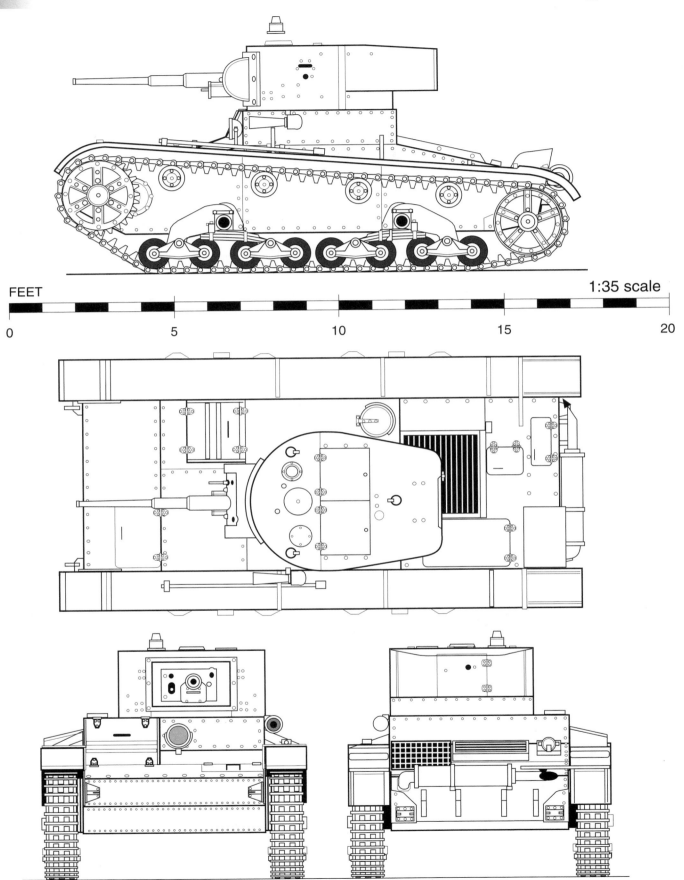

FEET

1:35 scale

0   5   10   15   20

T3E2 Christie Medium Tank
(Christie Model 1932 rebuilt by
America La-France for US Army tests)

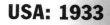

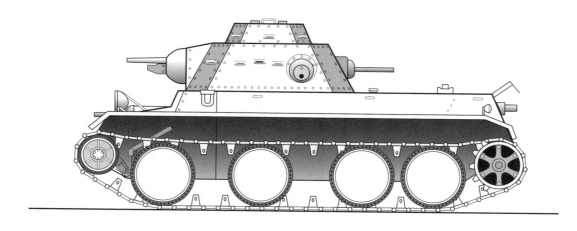

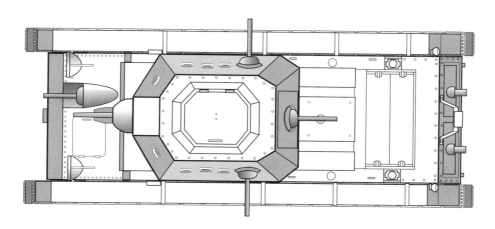

FEET

0   5   10   15   20

1:48 scale

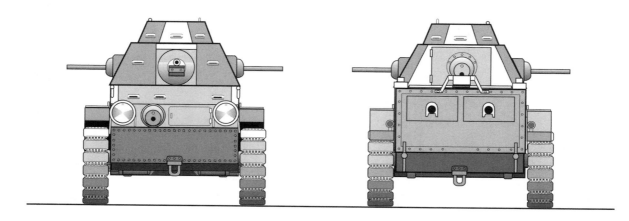

Vickers Medium Mark II**

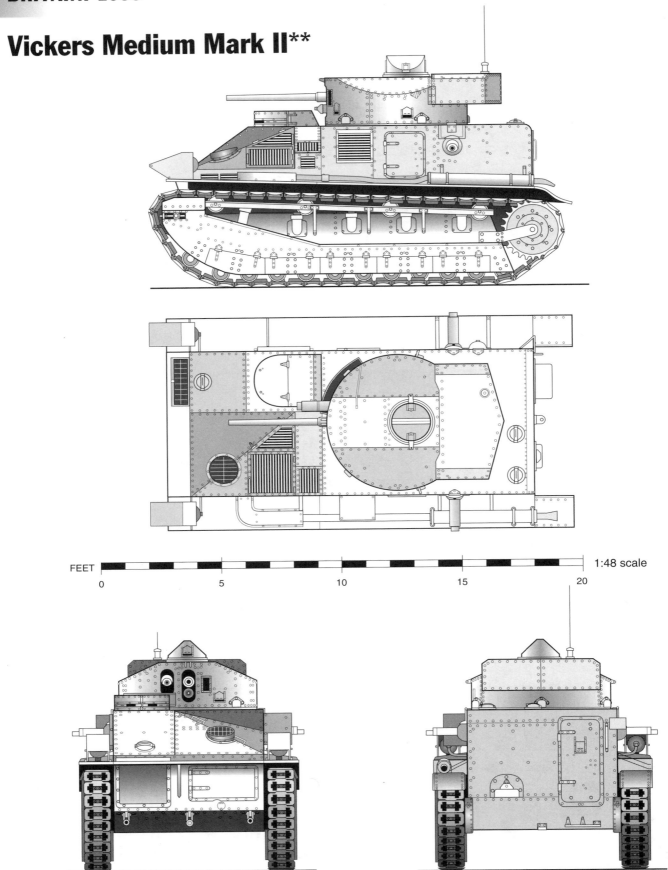

FEET 0 5 10 15 20   1:48 scale

T-26 Model 1933
Light Tank
(with final-production turret)

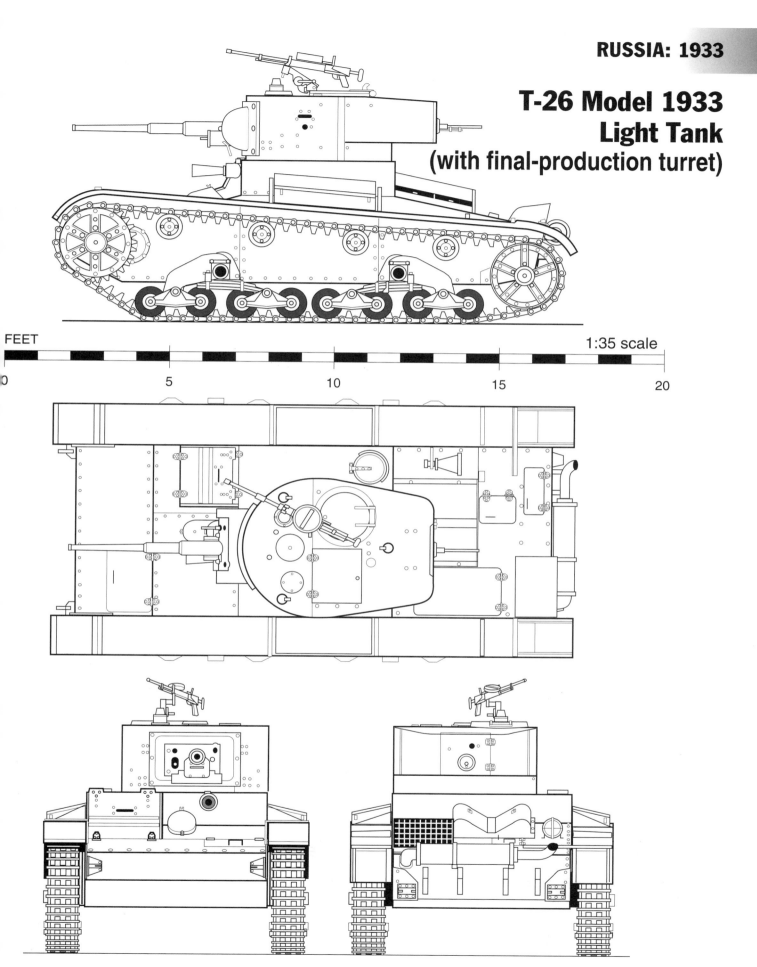

FEET

1:35 scale

0   5   10   15   20

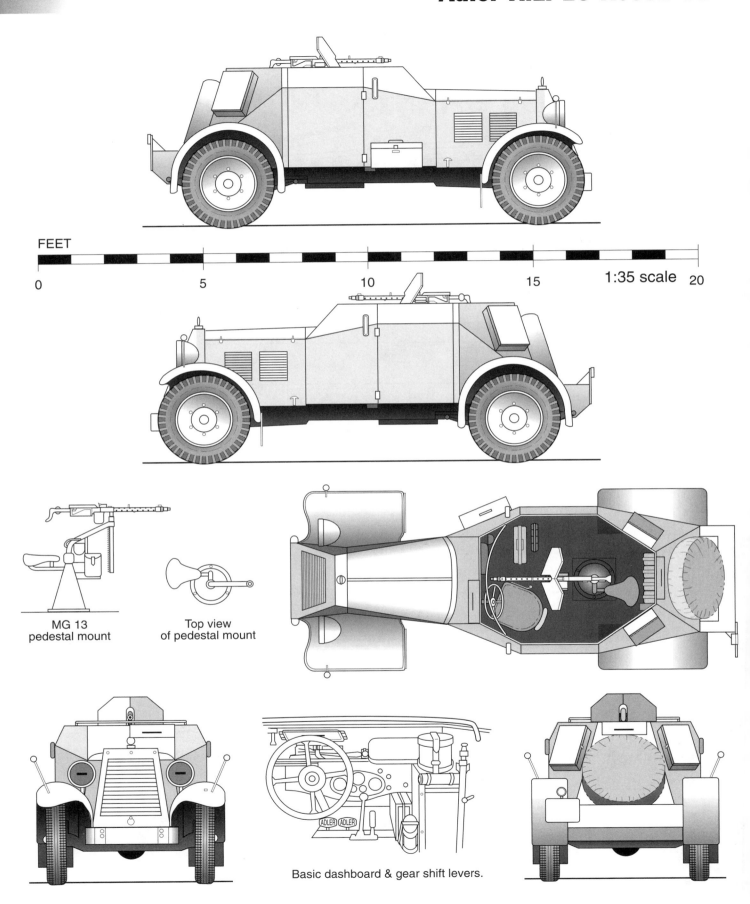

FEET

0 5 10 15 1:35 scale 20

MG 13
pedestal mount

Top view
of pedestal mount

Basic dashboard & gear shift levers.

C7P Artillery Tractor

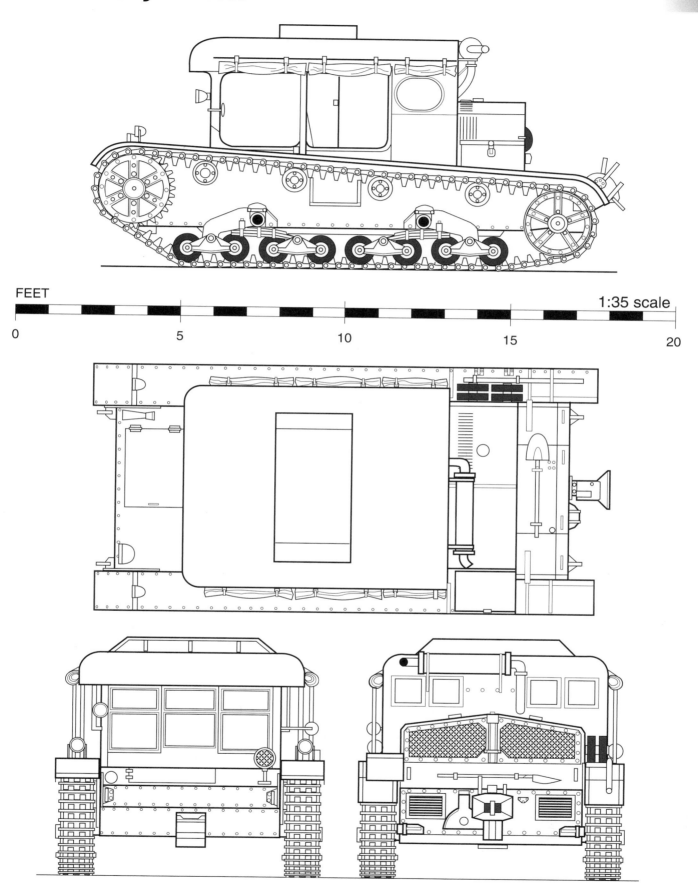

FEET

1:35 scale

0   5   10   15   20

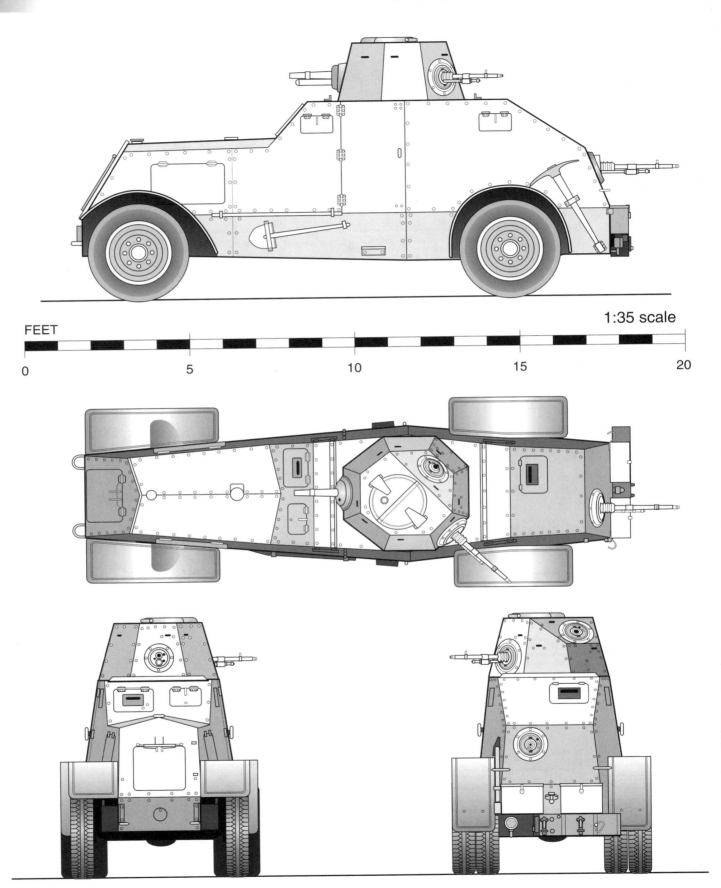

FEET

0   5   10   15   20

1:35 scale

Neubaufahrzeug
(Neubau-PzKpfw. IV)

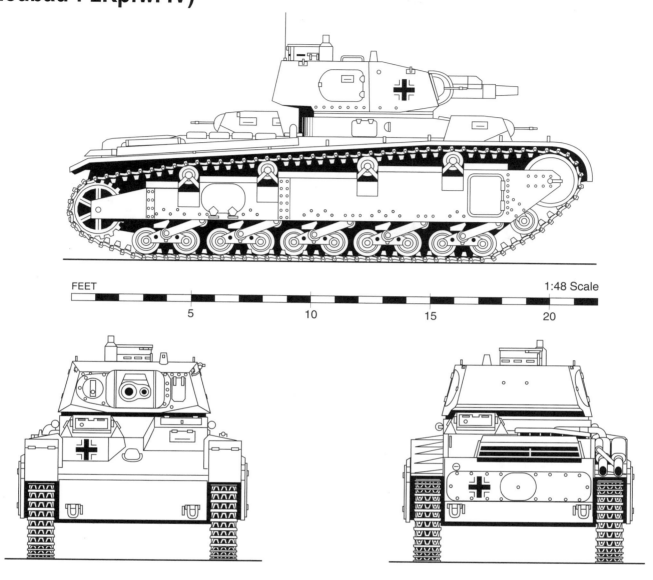

FEET

1:48 Scale

5   10   15   20

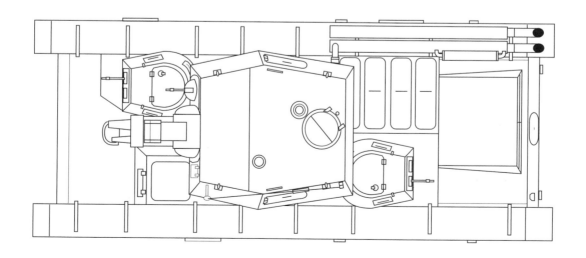

Carro Armato
L35/L.F. (lanciafiamme)
C.V. 33/II series fitted with flamethrower equipment

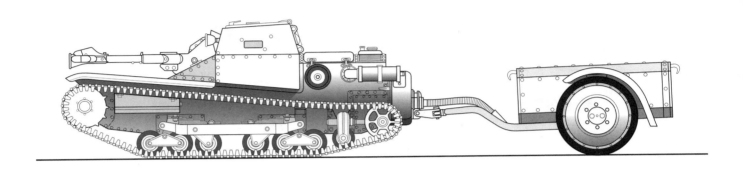

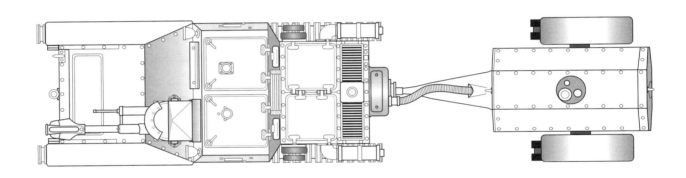

FEET

| 0 | 5 | 10 | 15 | 20 |

1:35 scale

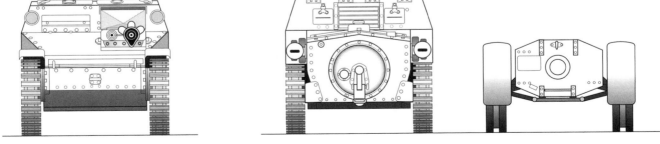

TKS Light Recon Tankette
fitted with 7.92mm machine gun

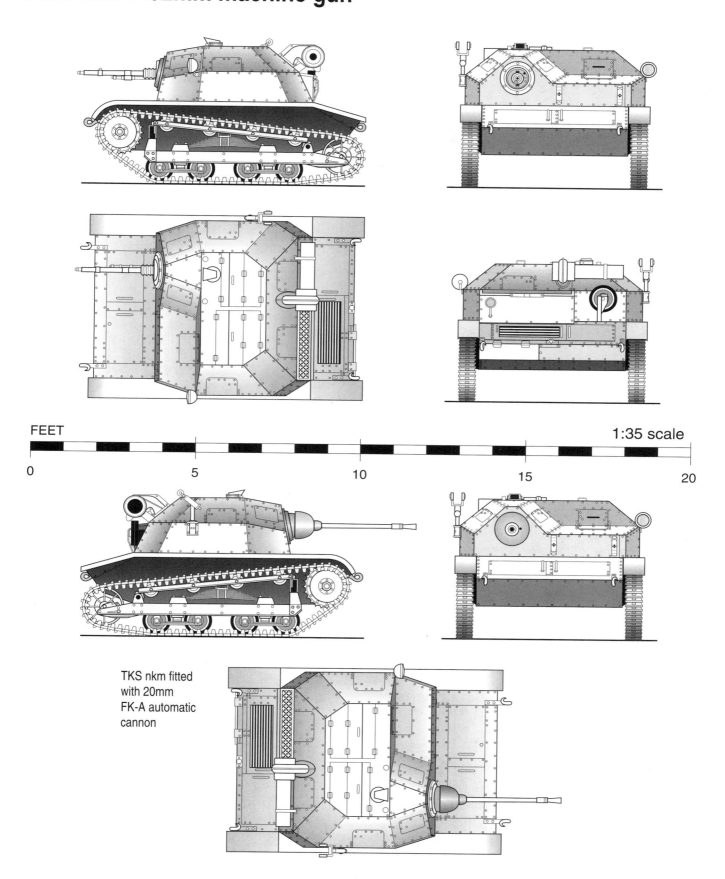

FEET

1:35 scale

0   5   10   15   20

TKS nkm fitted
with 20mm
FK-A automatic
cannon

BT-5 (Bystrochodyj Tank)
Model 1934 Fast Tank with standard-production turret

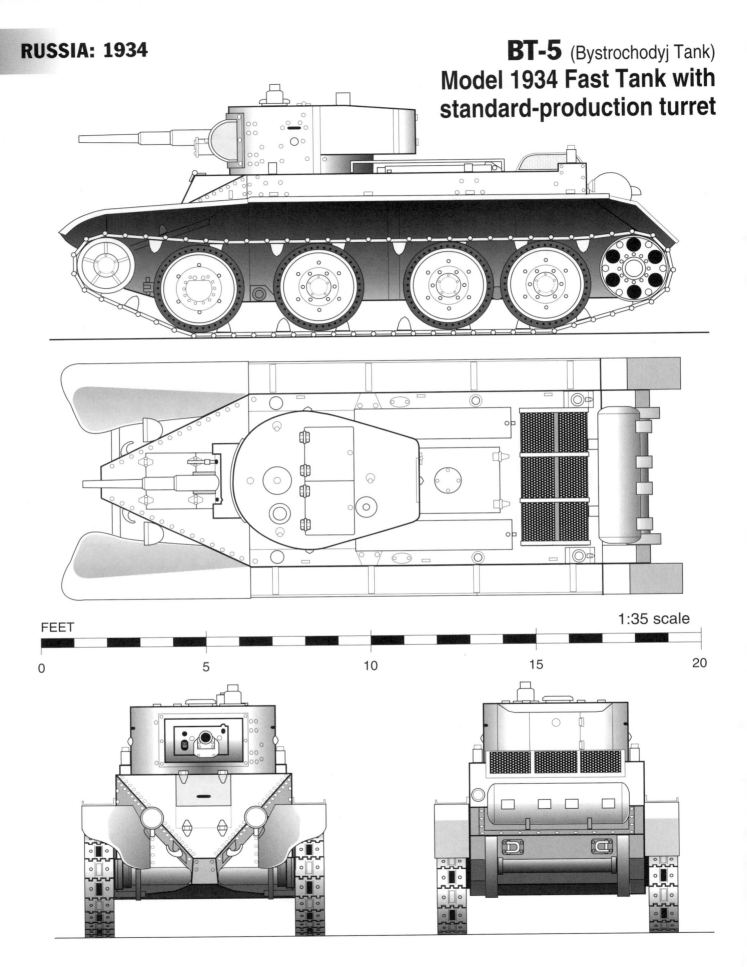

FEET

1:35 scale

0   5   10   15   20

Carden-Loyd Mark VI
Machine-gun Carrier

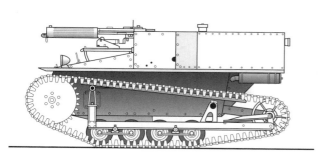

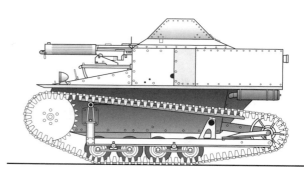

The basic Carden-Loyd Mk. VI with stowage boxes

The Carden-Loyd Mk. VI with armored headcovers,
supplied to Siam, USSR, Japan, Italy, S.America, and Asia.

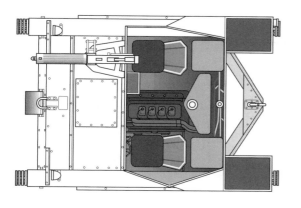

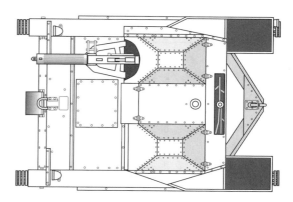

FEET

1:35 scale

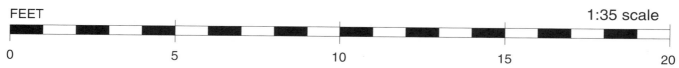

0 5 10 15 20

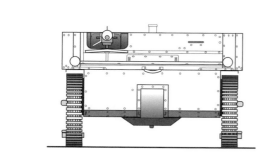

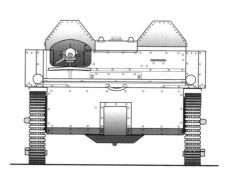

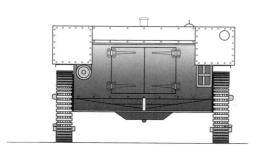

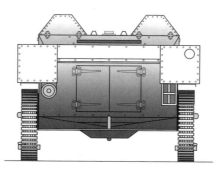

T-28 Heavy Tank
Model 1934

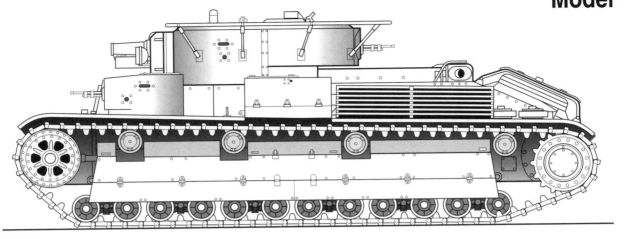

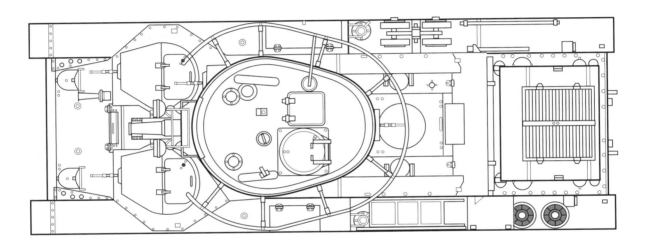

FEET

0   5   10   15   20

1:48 scale

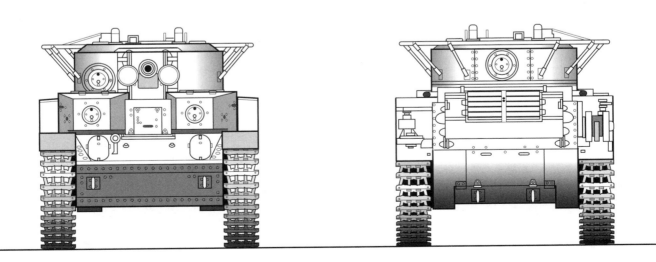

LT vz. 34 Light Tank
(P-II-R) Lehky tank vz. 34

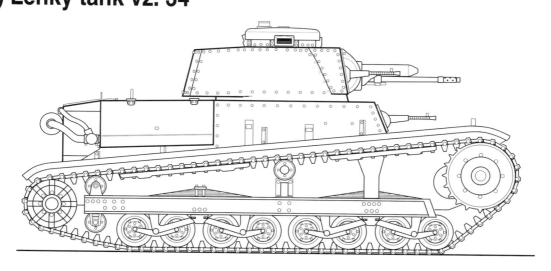

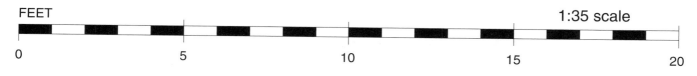

FEET

1:35 scale

0   5   10   15   20

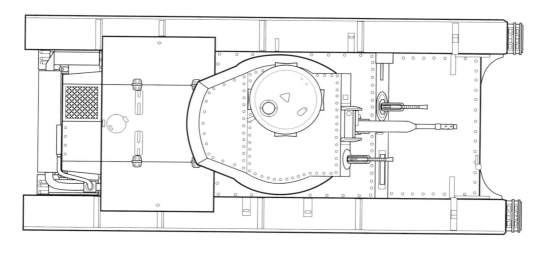

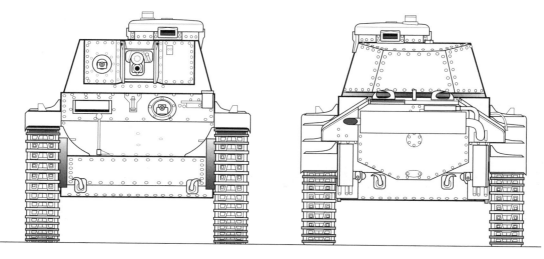

T13B2 Self-Propelled Gun
Auto Porté C 4,7 Type T13B2

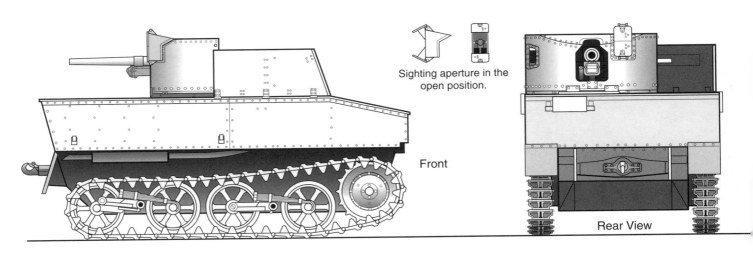

Sighting aperture in the open position.

Front

Rear View

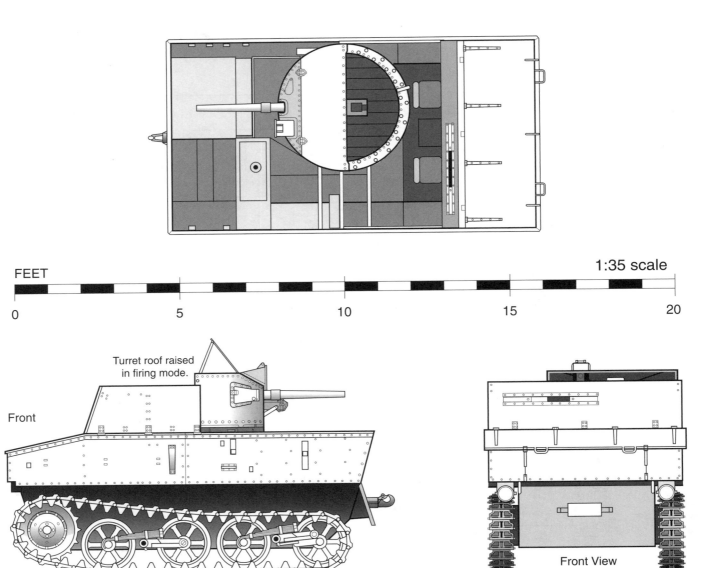

FEET

1:35 scale

0   5   10   15   20

Turret roof raised in firing mode.

Front

Front View

M1 Armored Car
(T4 Standardized)

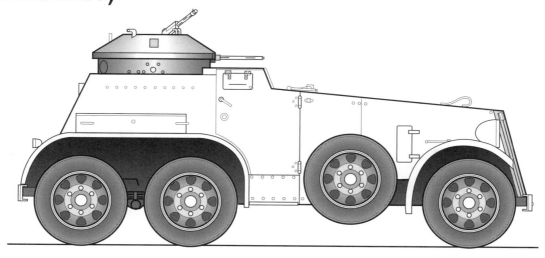

FEET   1:35 scale

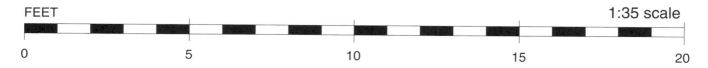

0   5   10   15   20

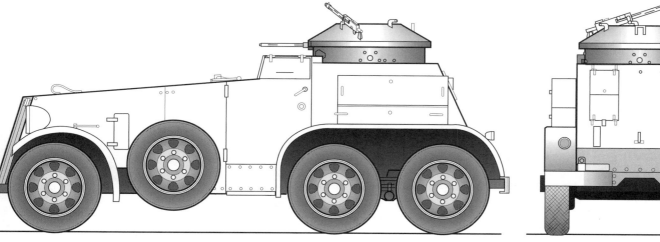

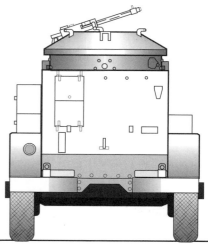

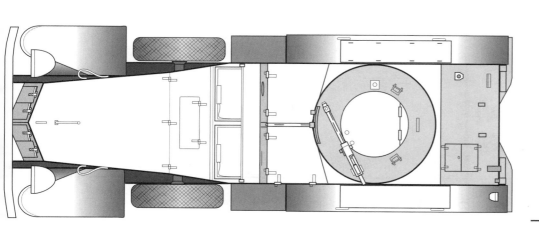

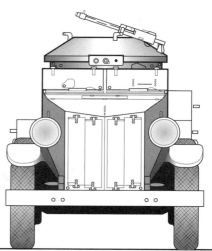

Renault UE Supply Carrier
Chenillette de ravaillment d'infanterie

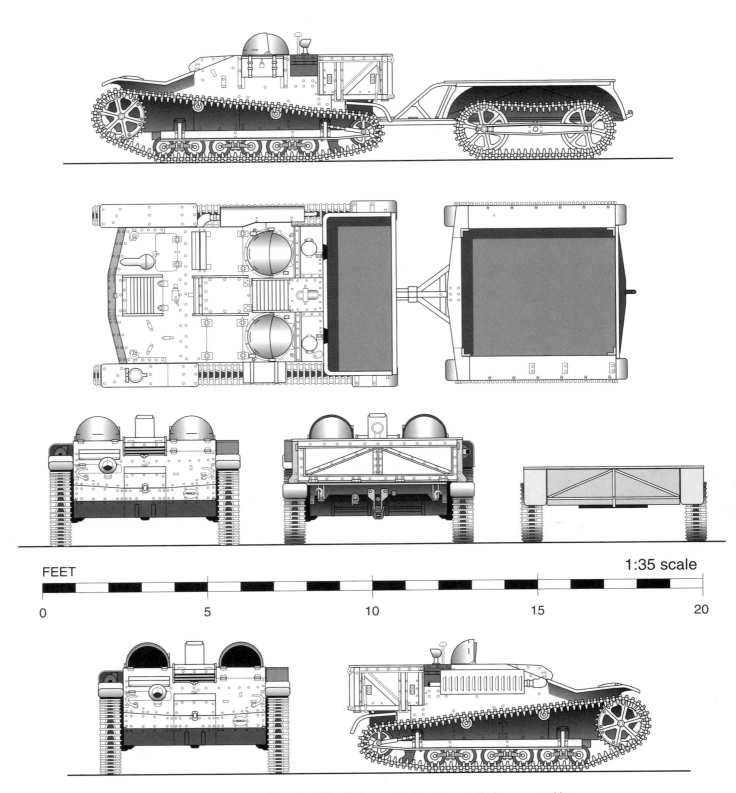

FEET

0   5   10   15   20

1:35 scale

These two views show the UE with the conical hatches in their open position.

T15 Light Tank
Vickers-Carden-Loyd
1934

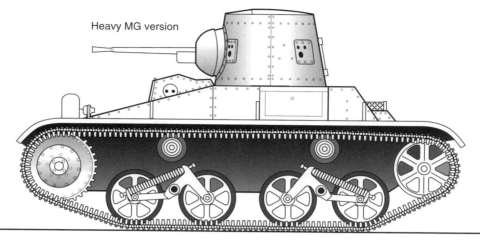

Heavy MG version

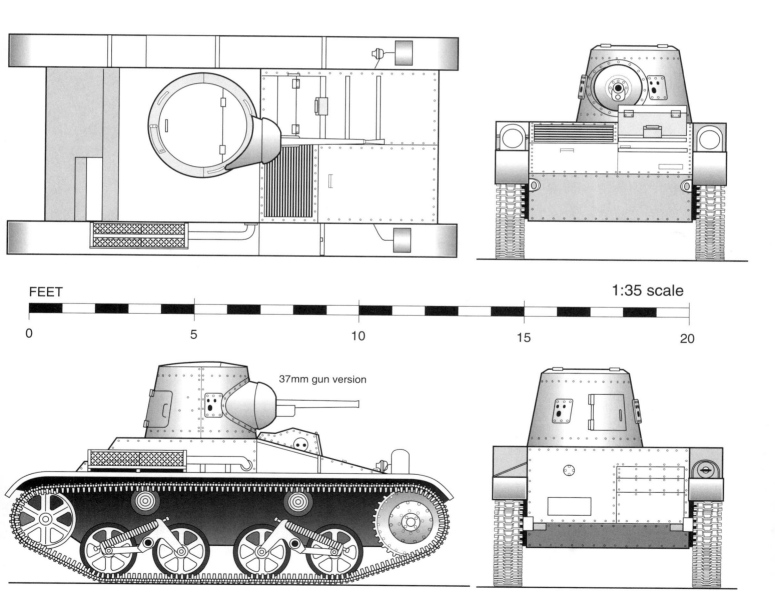

FEET

1:35 scale

0   5   10   15   20

37mm gun version

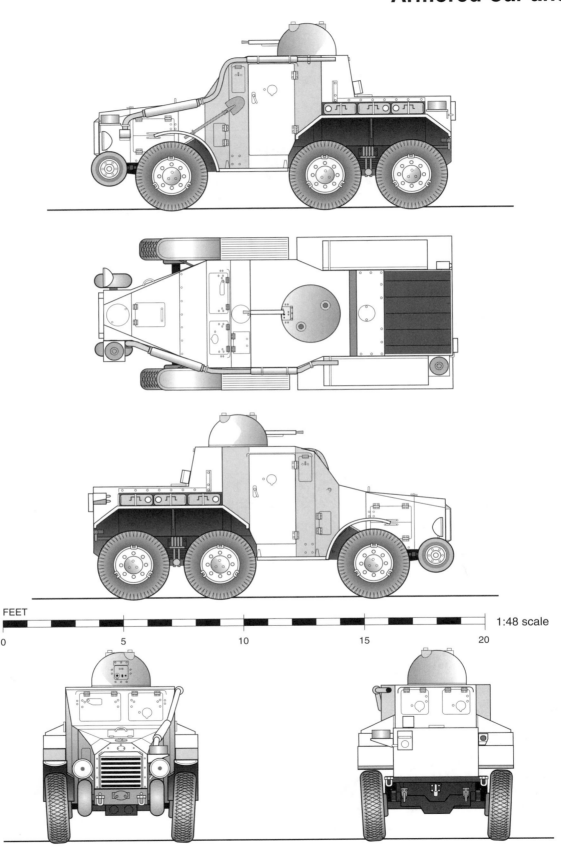

FEET   1:48 scale

0   5   10   15   20

LT vz. 35 Light Tank (T-11)
(Skoda/CKD S-II-a)

FEET

1:35 scale

0   5   10   15   20

Schwerer Panzerspähwagen
Sd.Kfz. 231 (6-rad)

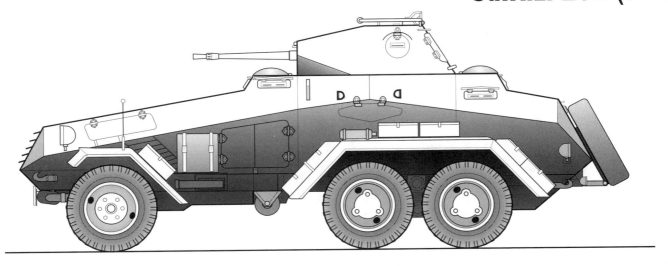

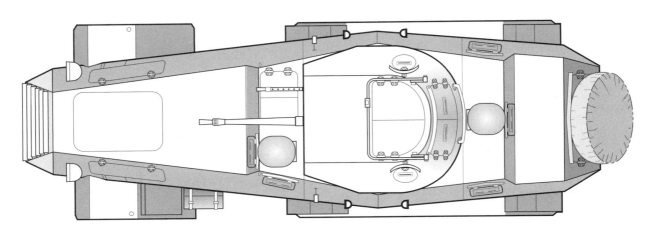

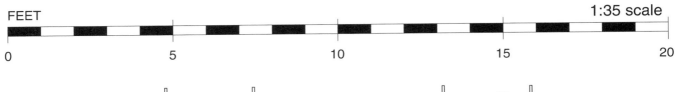

FEET

1:35 scale

0   5   10   15   20

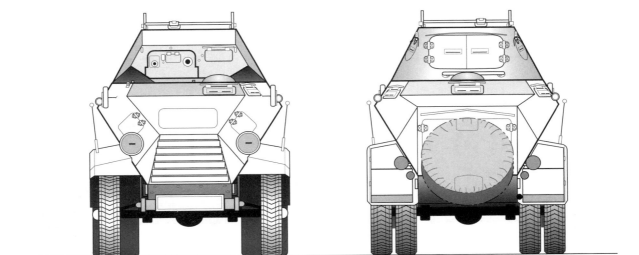

AMD Panhard 178 Modèle 1935 Armored Car

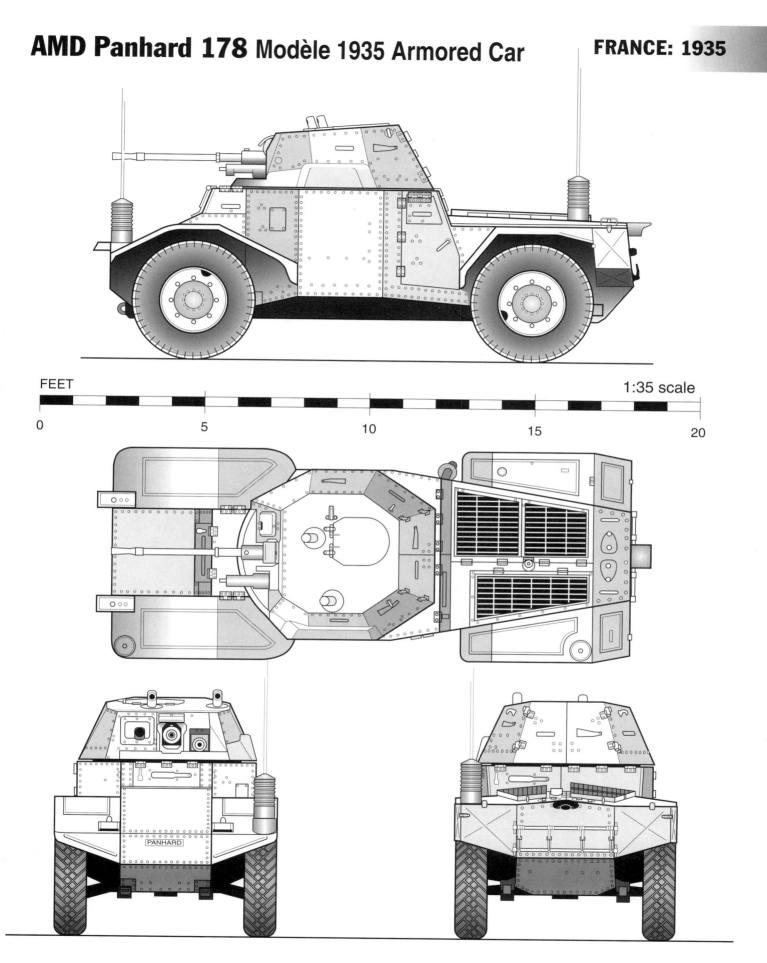

FEET

1:35 scale

0   5   10   15   20

PANHARD

AMC Renault 1935 ACG-1
Light Tank

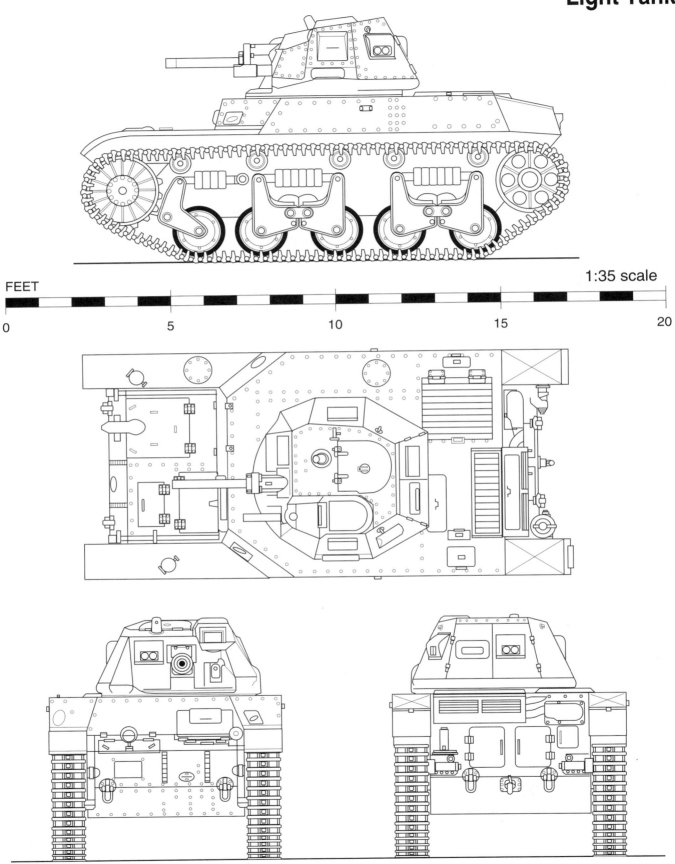

1:35 scale

FEET

0   5   10   15   20

Sd.Kfz. 221 Armored Car

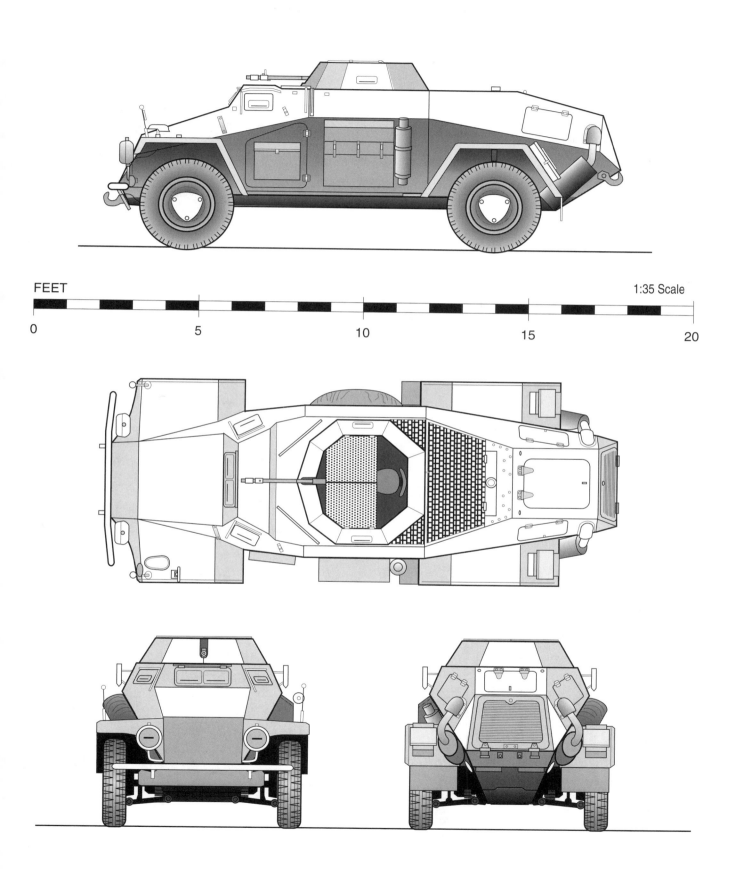

FEET

1:35 Scale

0   5   10   15   20

AMD Laffly 80 AM
Laffly-Vincennes
Armored Car

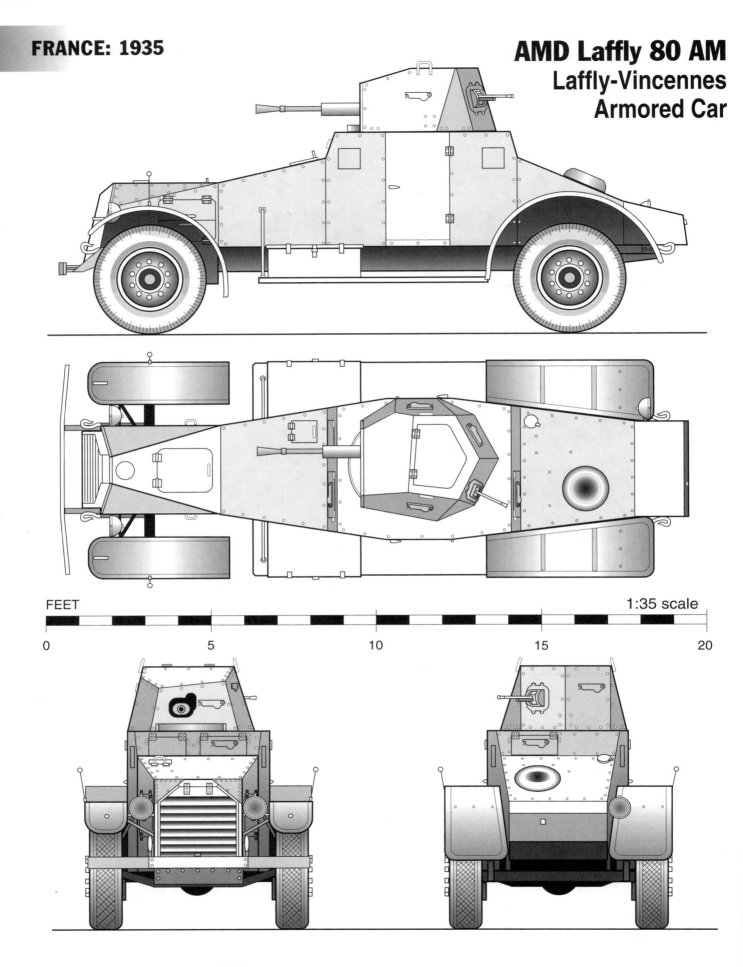

FEET   1:35 scale

0   5   10   15   20

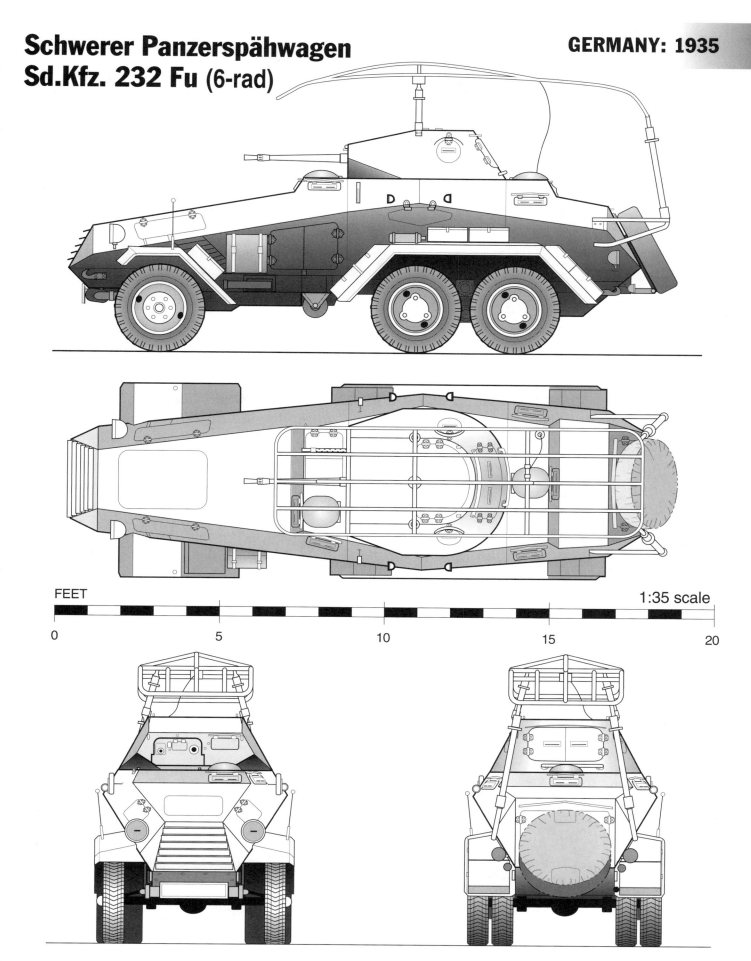

Schwerer Panzerspähwagen
Sd.Kfz. 232 Fu (6-rad)

FEET

1:35 scale

0   5   10   15   20

Renault R-35 Light Tank
(Char lèger Mle 1935 R)

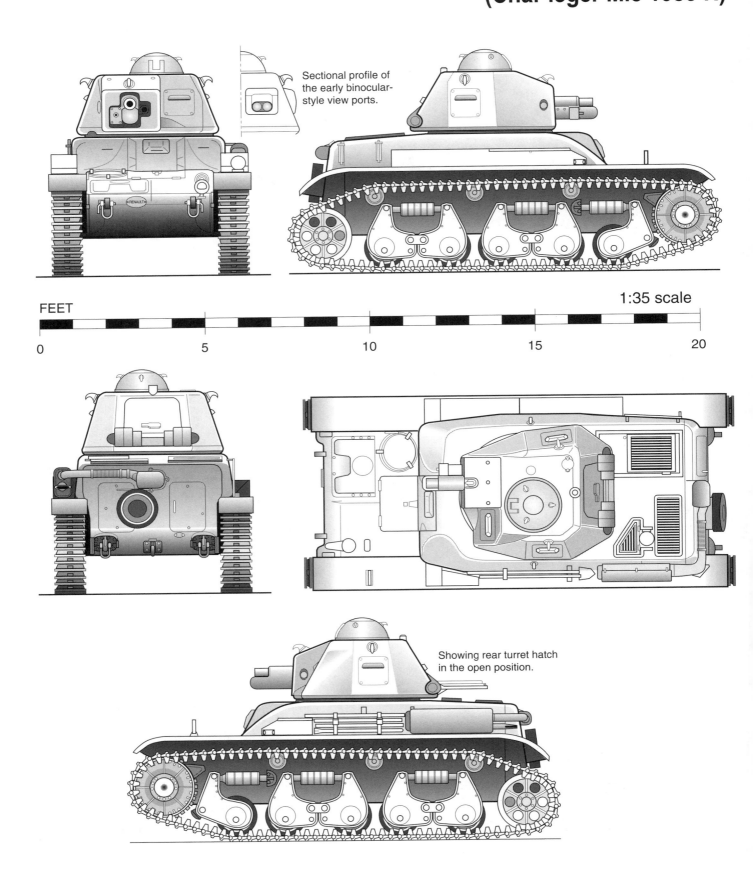

Sectional profile of the early binocular-style view ports.

1:35 scale

FEET

0   5   10   15   20

Showing rear turret hatch in the open position.

T13B3 Self-Propelled Anti-Tank Gun
Autocanon 4,7 Type T13B3

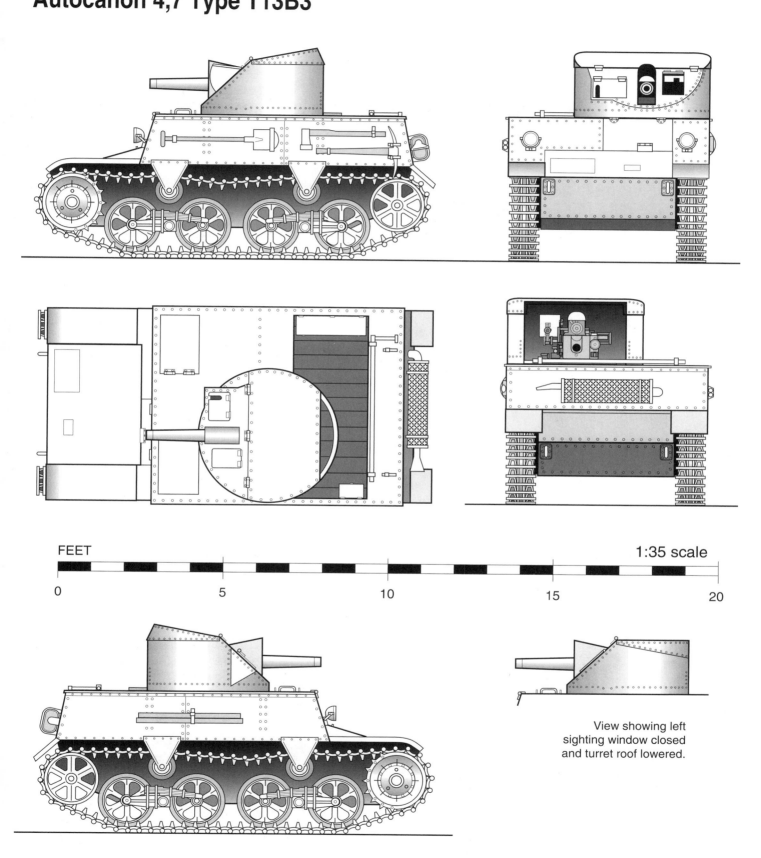

FEET

1:35 scale

0   5   10   15   20

View showing left
sighting window closed
and turret roof lowered.

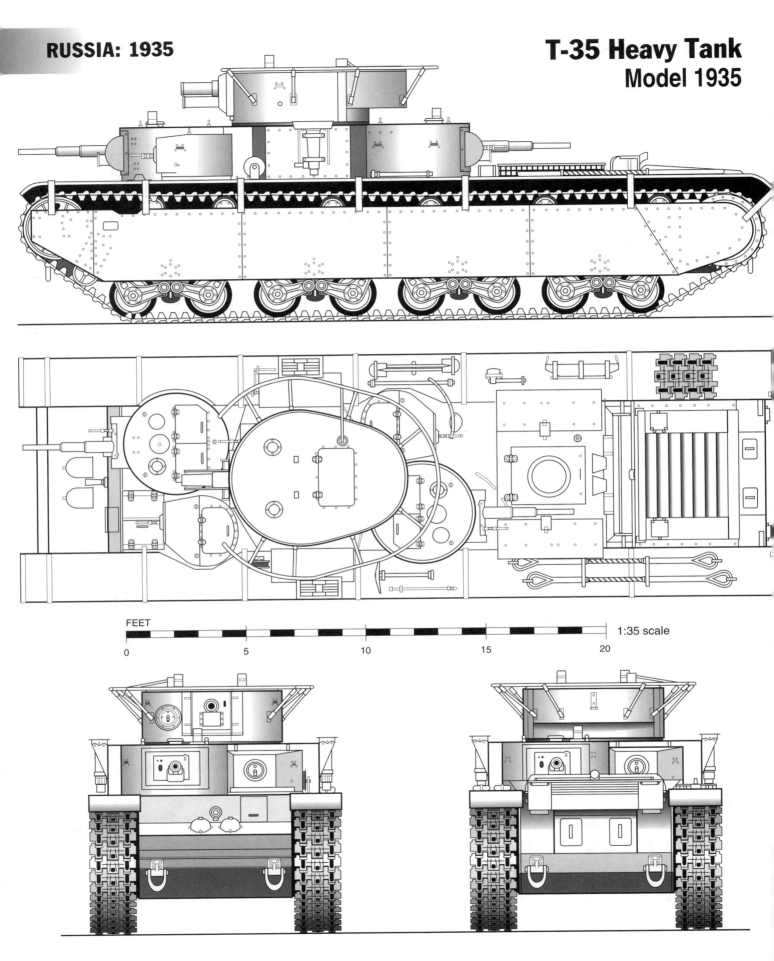

FEET

1:35 scale

0 5 10 15 20

Pz.Kpfw. I Ausf. A Light Tank
(Sd. Kfz. 101)

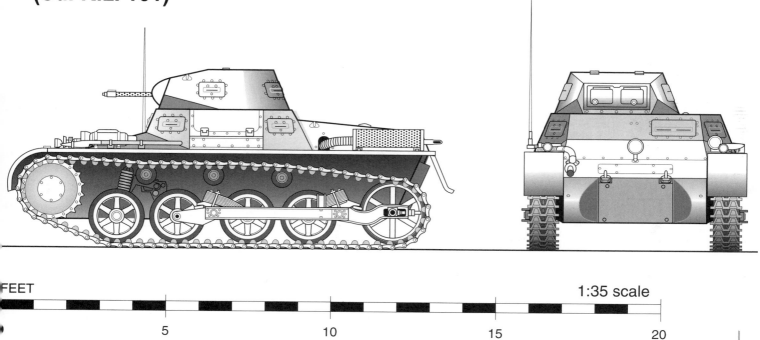

FEET

1:35 scale

5   10   15   20

Shown with aerial stowed in the travel position.

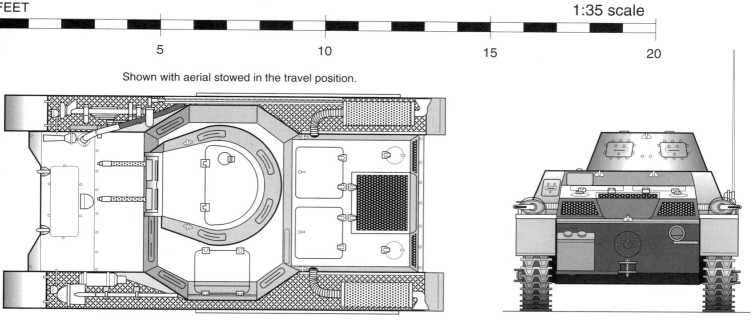

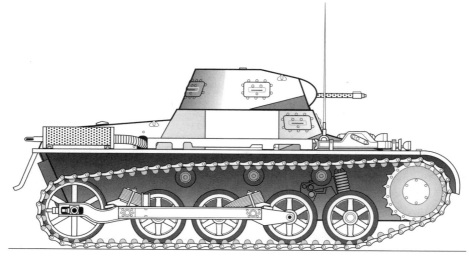

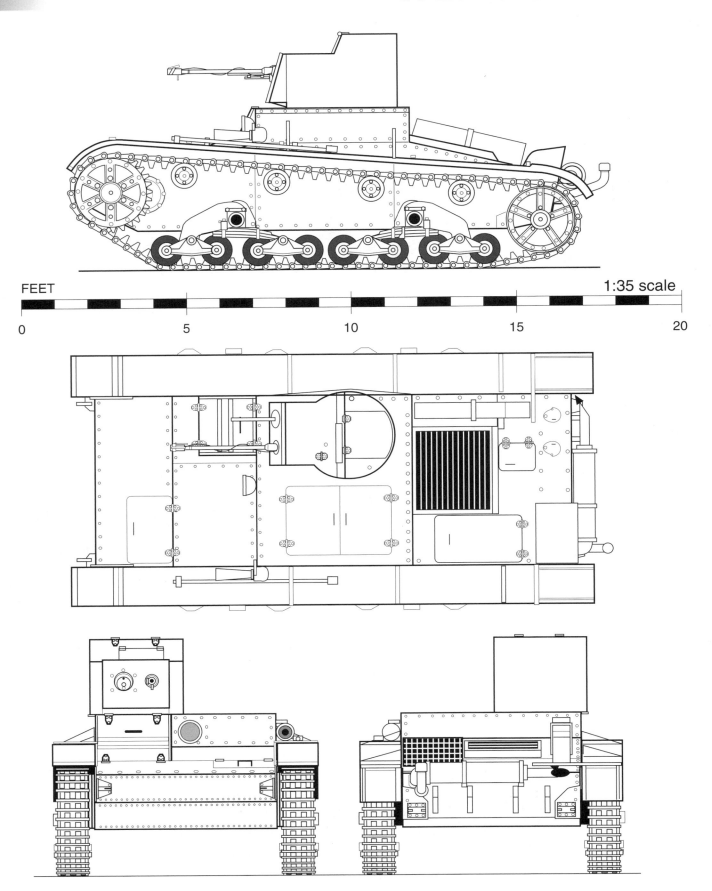

FEET

1:35 scale

0   5   10   15   20

FCM 36 Light Tank
(Char lèger Modèle 1936 FCM)

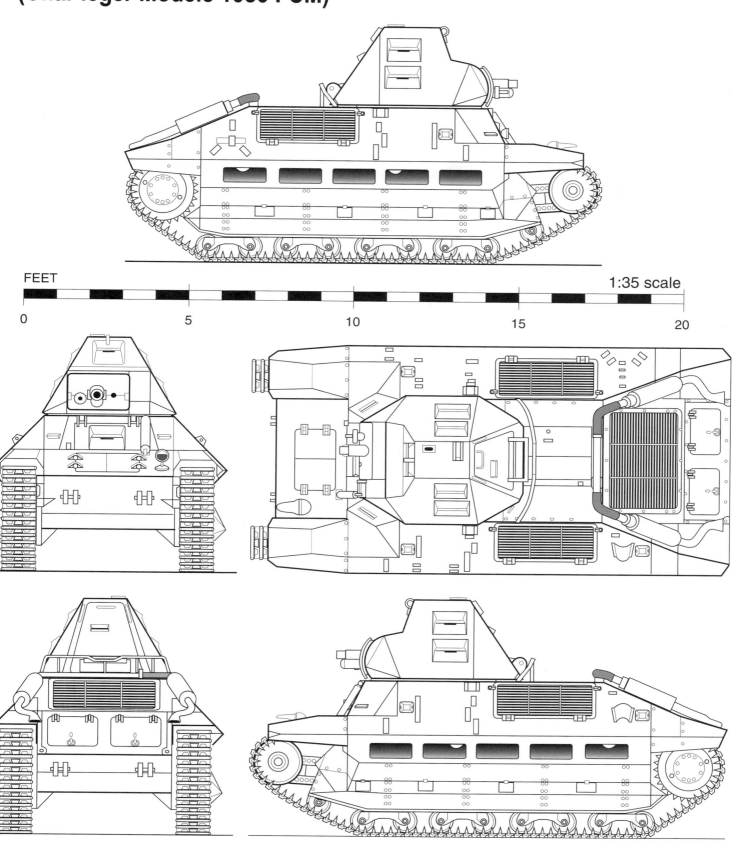

FEET

1:35 scale

0   5   10   15   20

Mark VIA
Light Tank

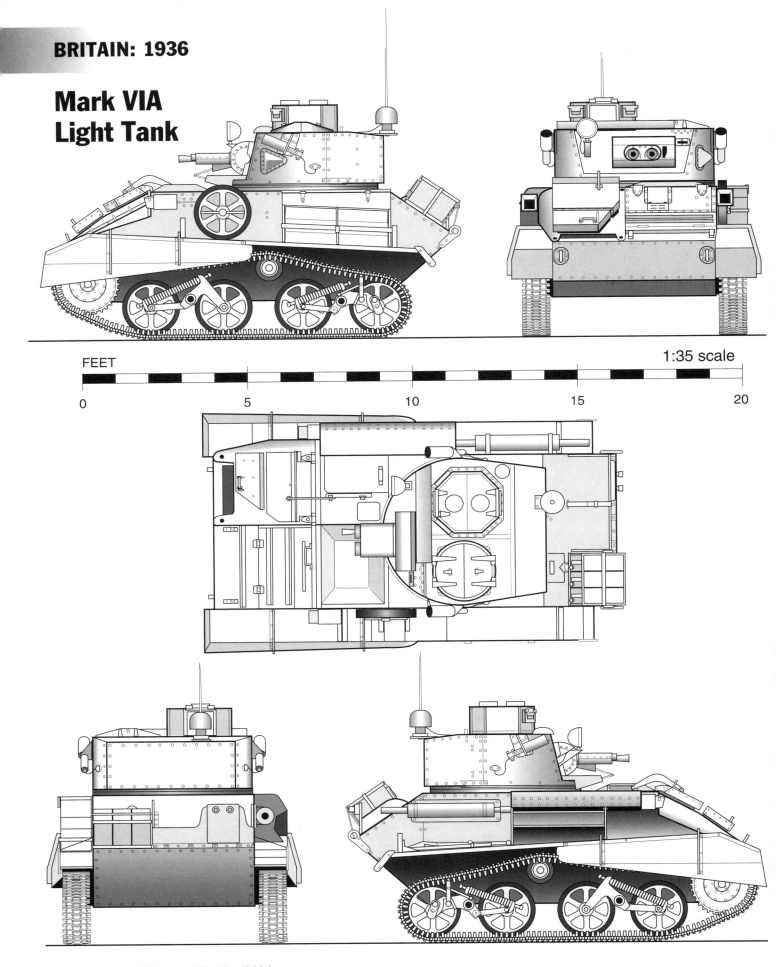

FEET

0   5   10   15   20

1:35 scale

Kleiner Panzerbefehlswagen
(Sd. Kfz. 265) Version 3K1B Light Armored Command Vehicle

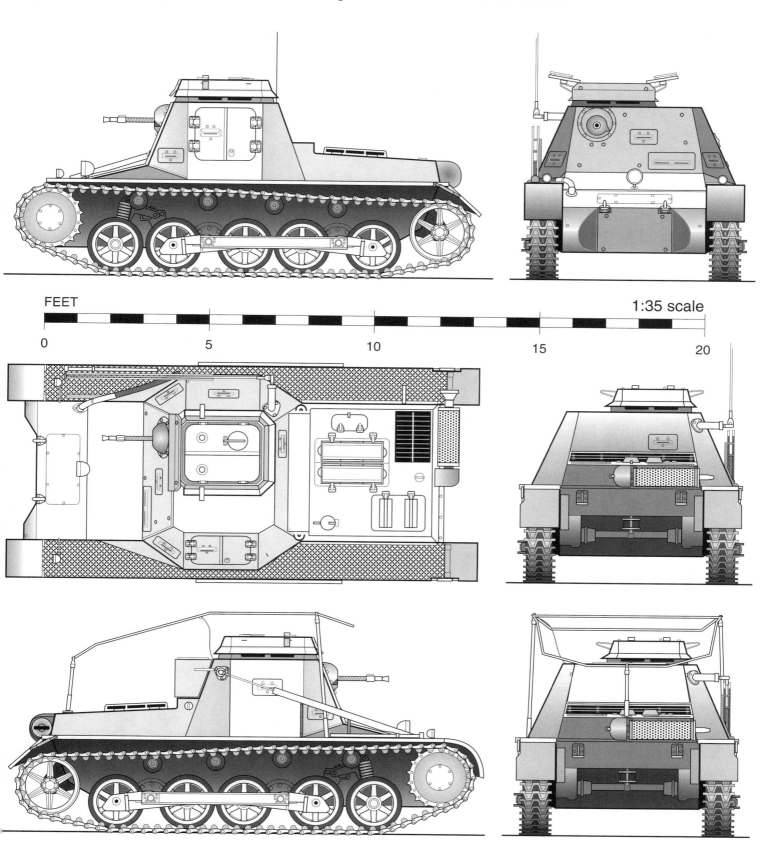

FEET

1:35 scale

0   5   10   15   20

Matilda Mark I Infantry Tank (A11)

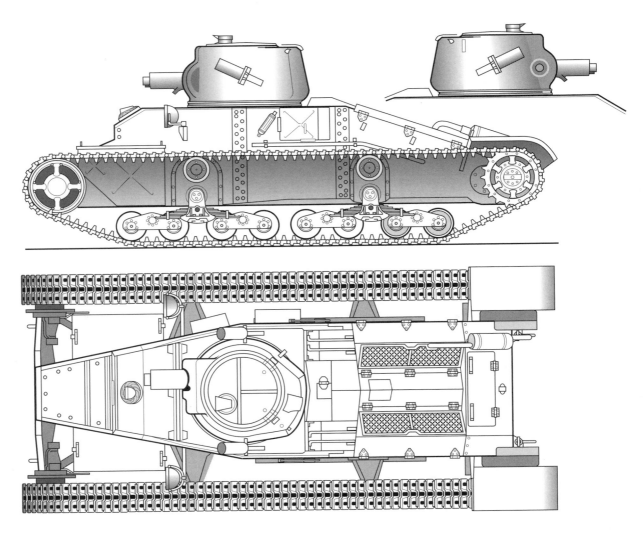

FEET

1:35 scale

0   5   10   15   20

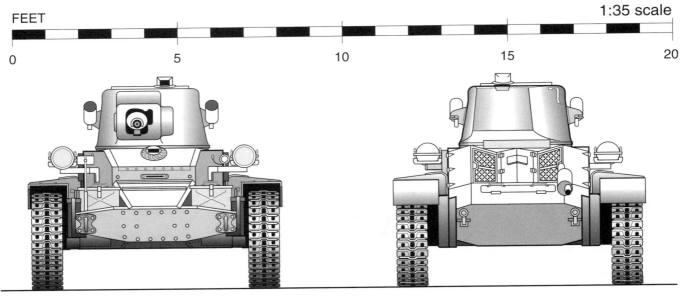

Pantserwagen M.36 (L180)
6x4 Heavy Armored Car

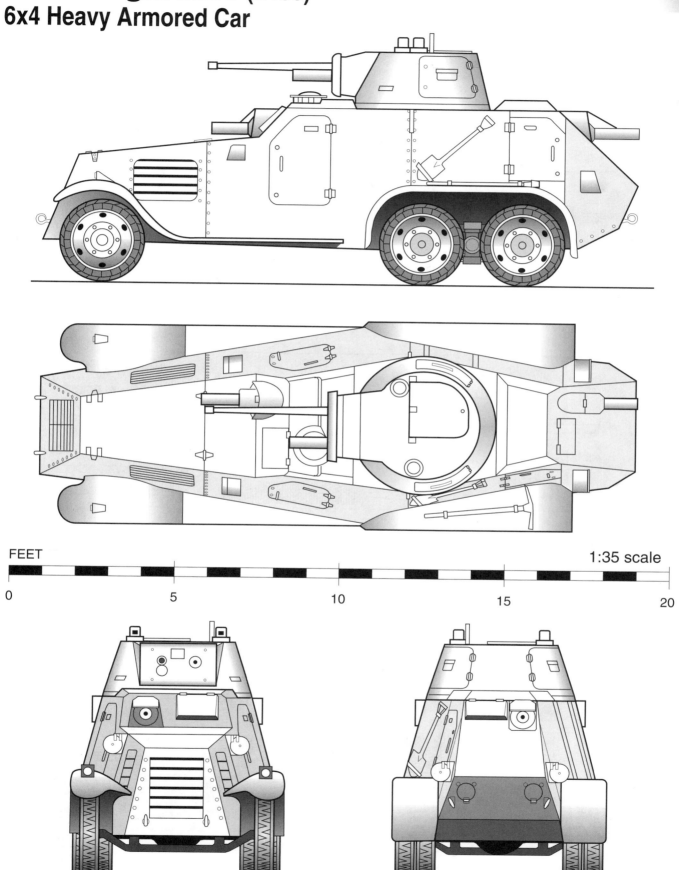

FEET

1:35 scale

0 5 10 15 20

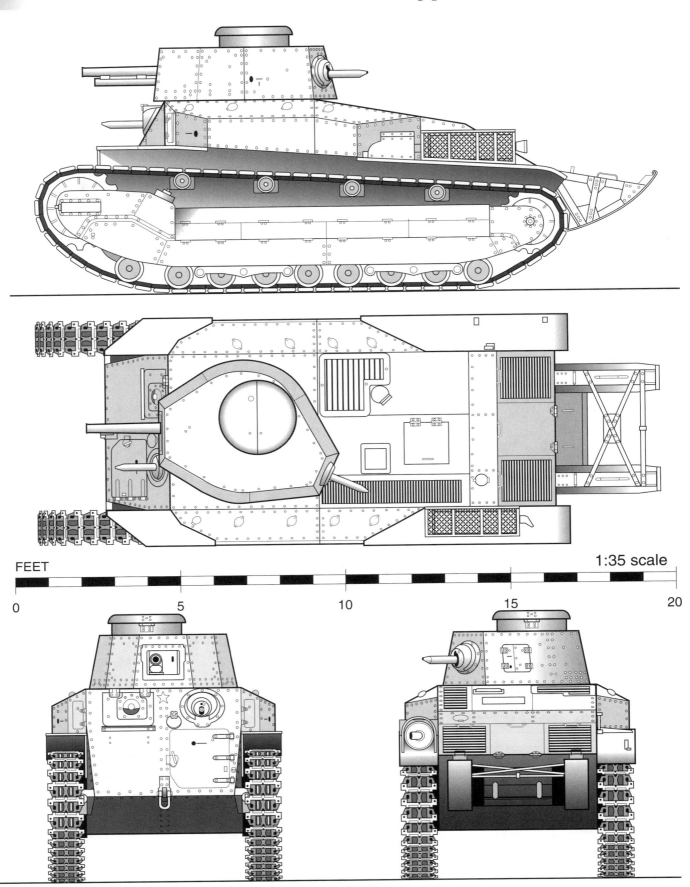

FEET

1:35 scale

0   5   10   15   20

SOMUA S35
Medium Tank

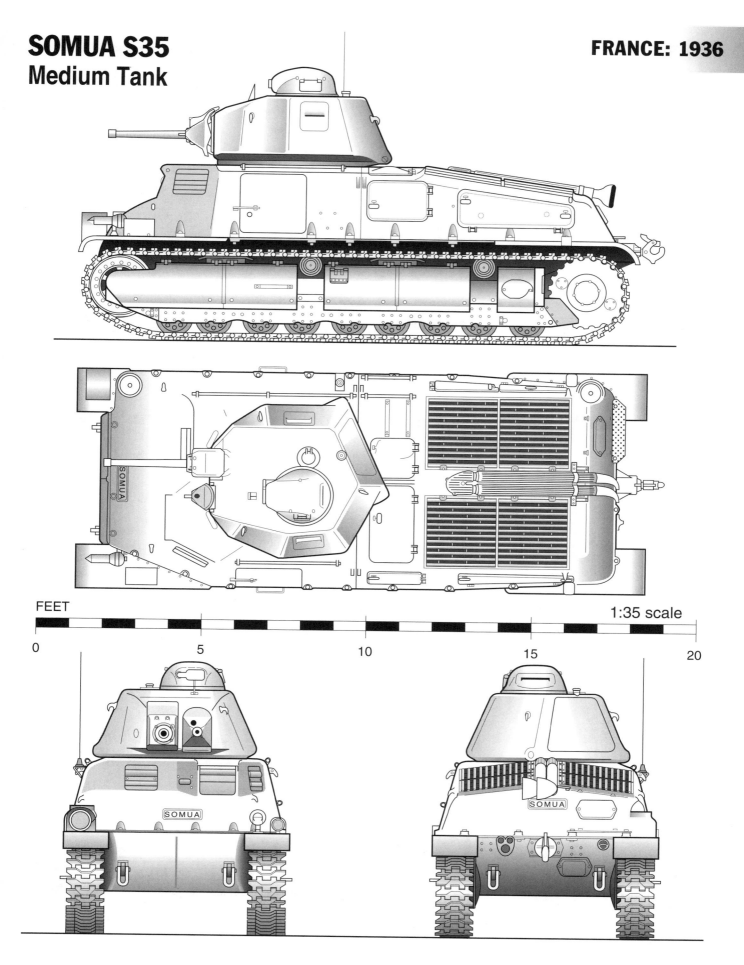

FEET

1:35 scale

0   5   10   15   20

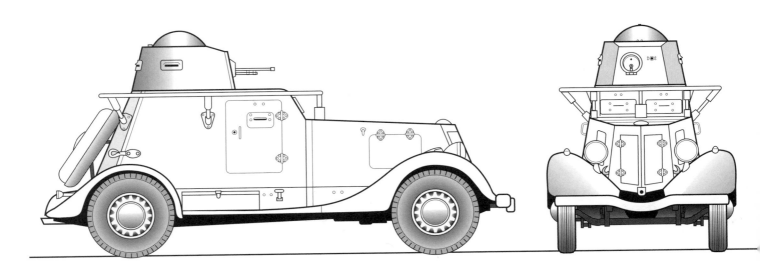

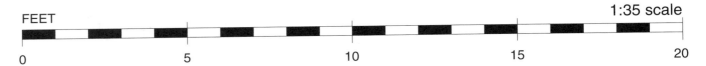

FEET

1:35 scale

0   5   10   15   20

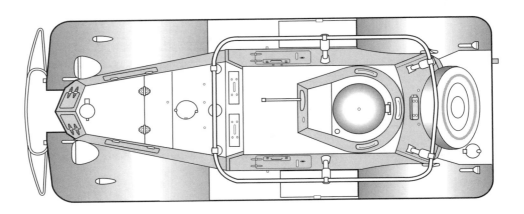

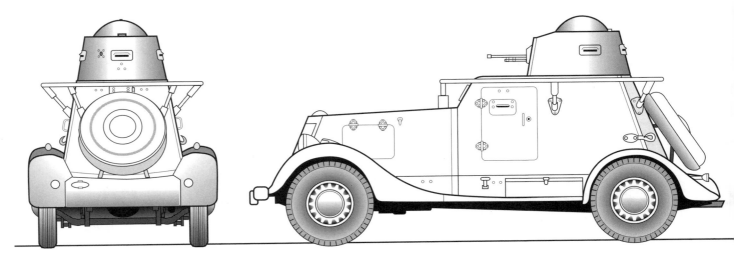

M1 Combat Car

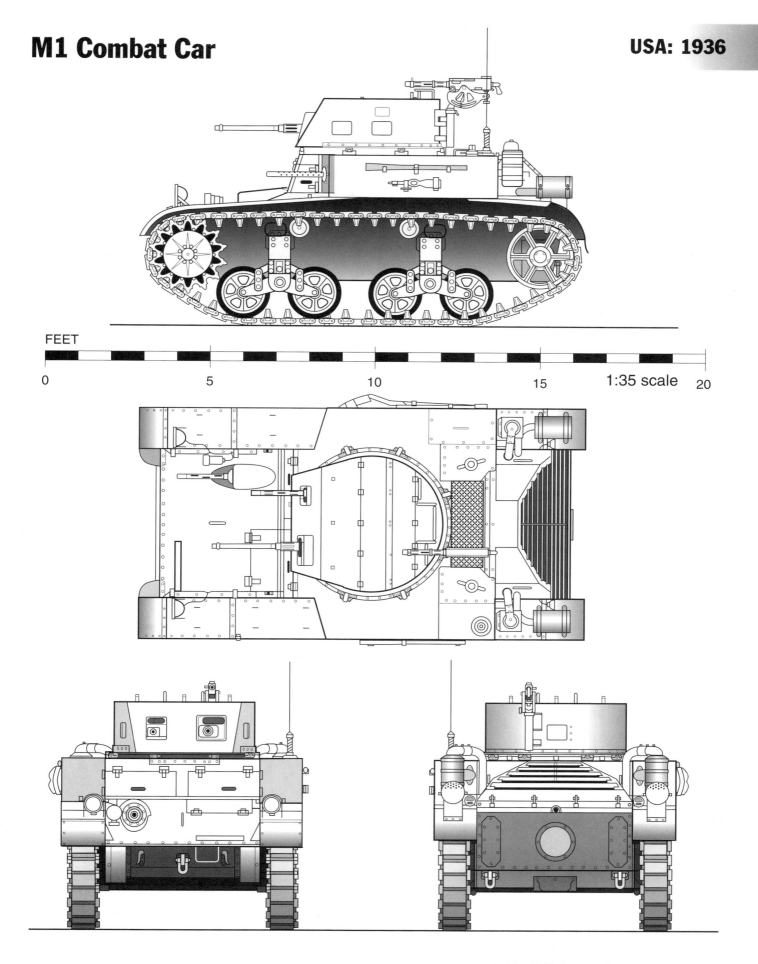

FEET

0   5   10   15   1:35 scale   20

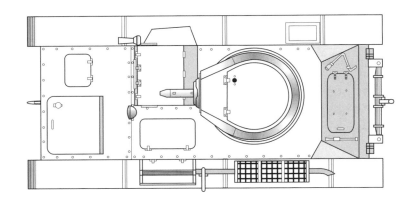

FEET

1:35 scale

0   5   10   15   20

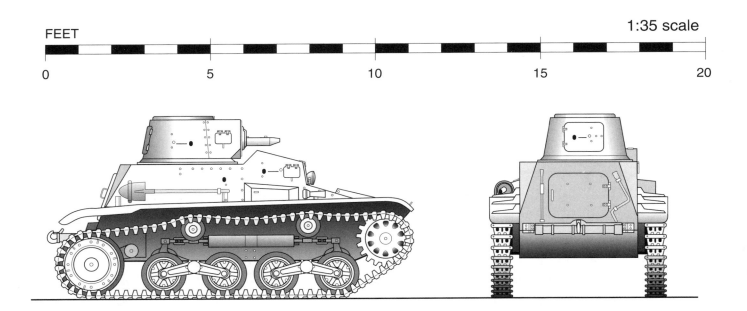

Type 97 Te-Ke Tankette

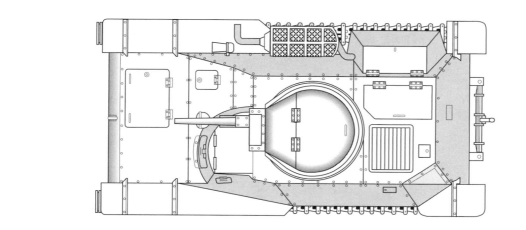

FEET

1:35 scale

0   5   10   15   20

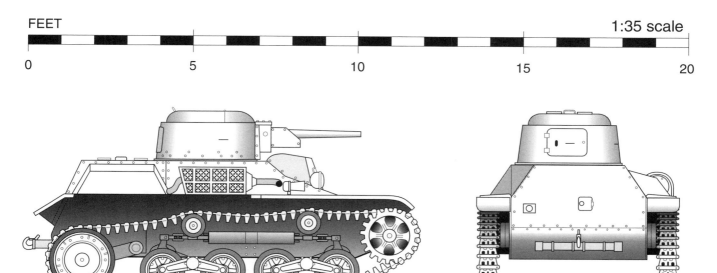

Mark VIB Light Tank

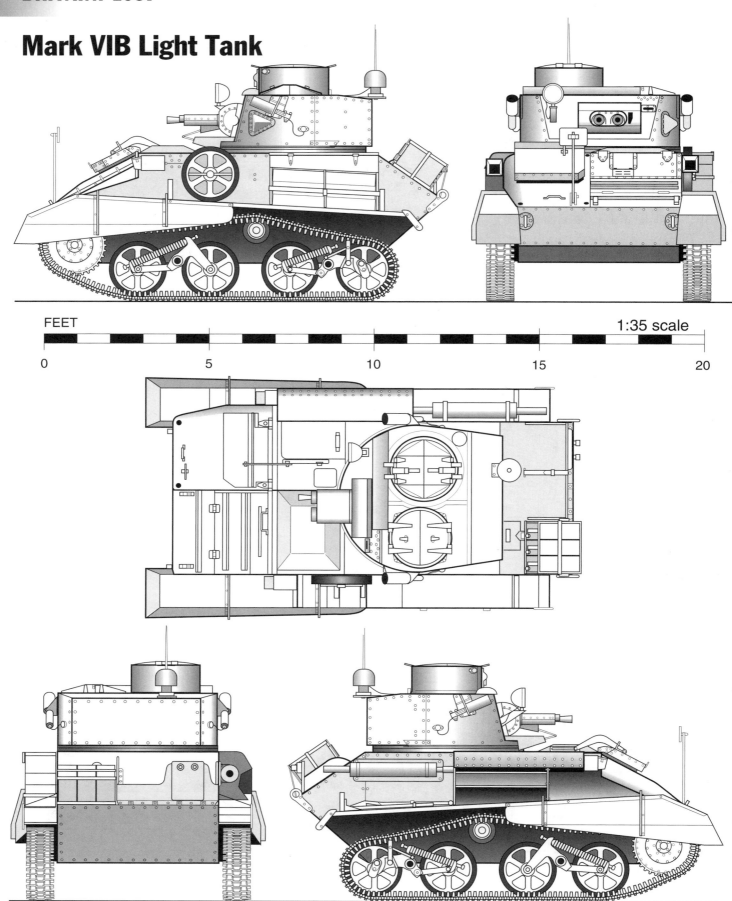

FEET

1:35 scale

0   5   10   15   20

T-38 Model 1937
Light Amphibious Tank

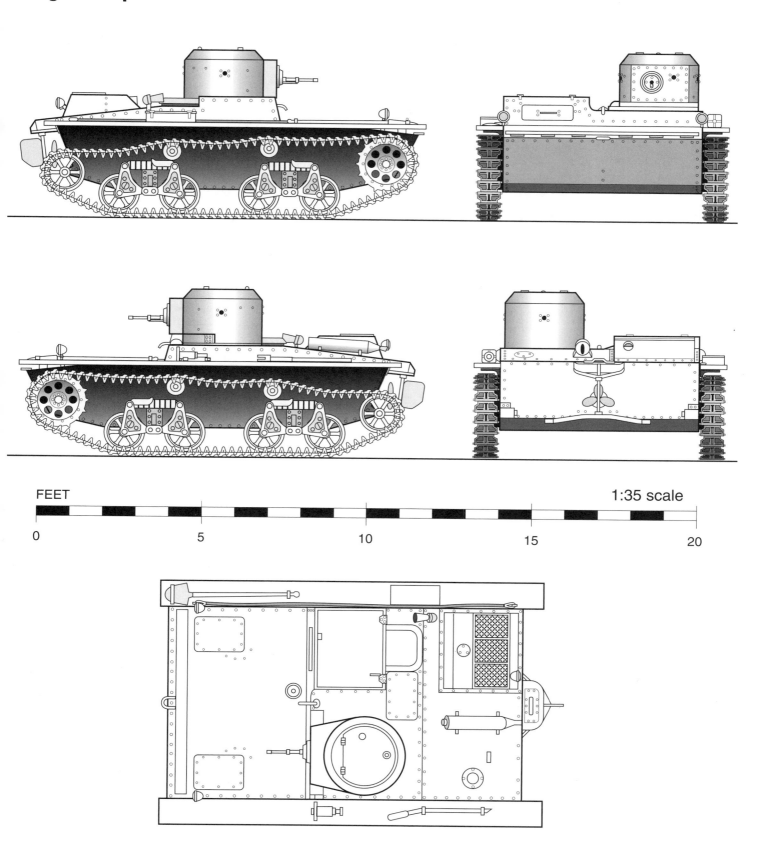

FEET

1:35 scale

0   5   10   15   20

Laffly type W15 TCC
Chasseur de chars (47mm modèle 1937 gun)

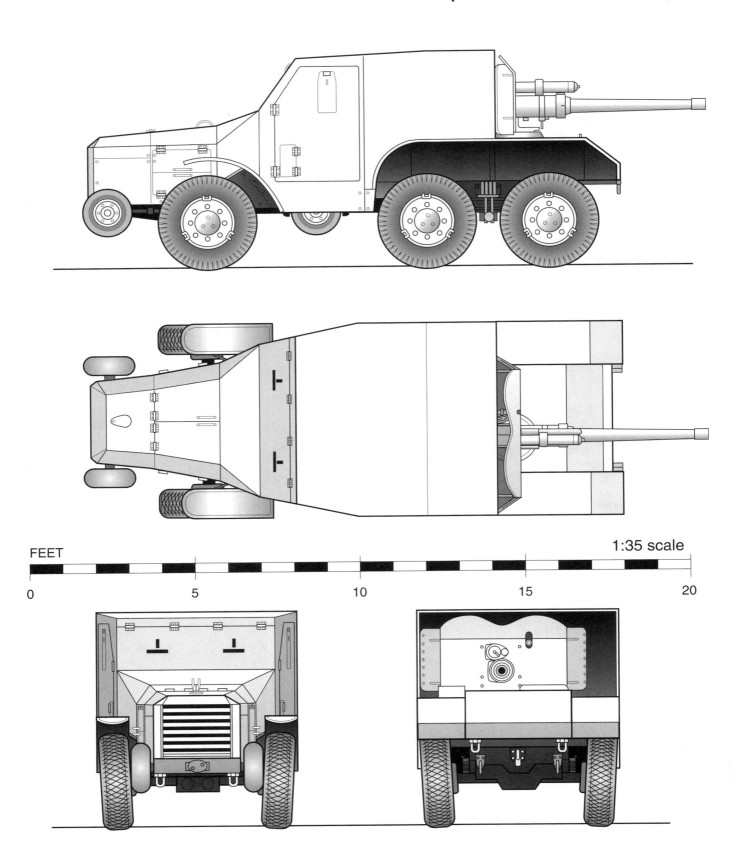

FEET

1:35 scale

0   5   10   15   20

R-1 Tankette
(Czech export of CKD tankette AH-IV)

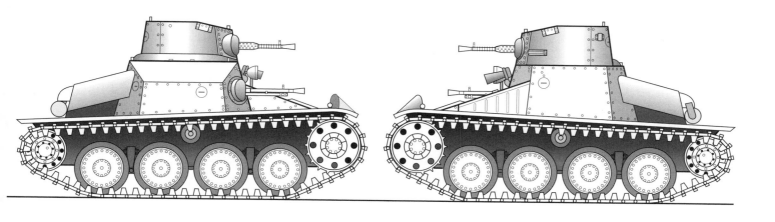

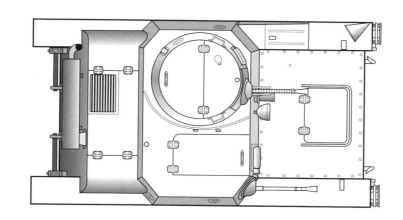

FEET

1:35 scale

0   5   10   15   20

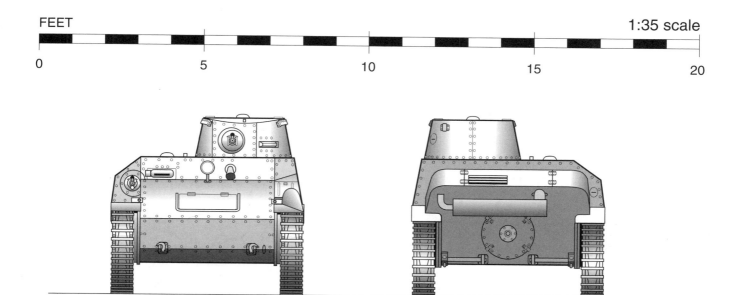

R-2 Light Tank
(Skoda Light Tank R-2)

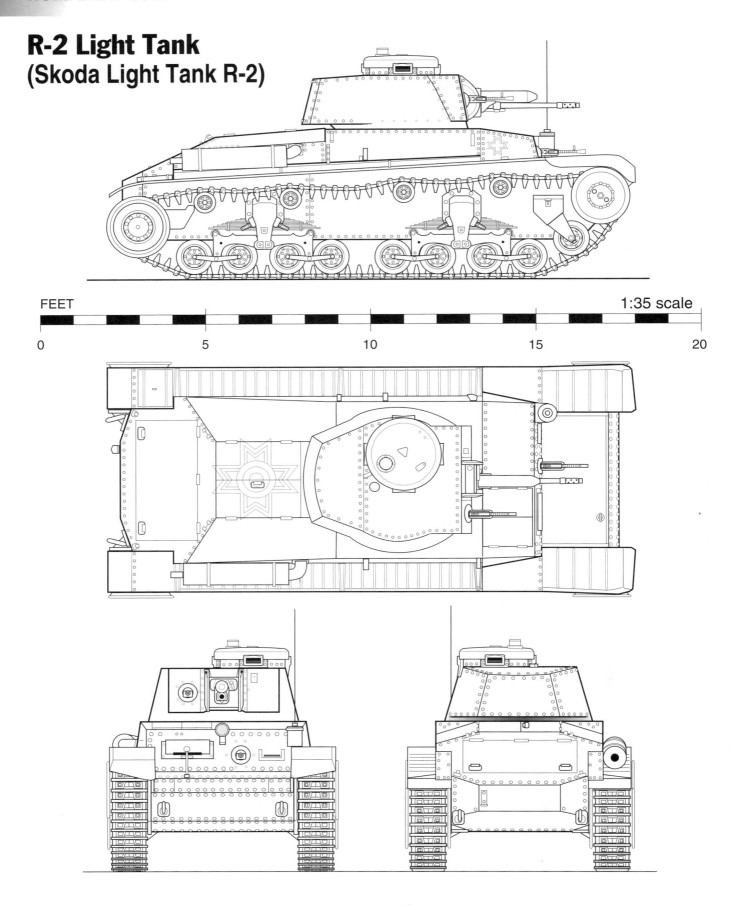

FEET

1:35 scale

0   5   10   15   20

Pz.Kpfw. I Ausf. B early (Sd. Kfz. 101)

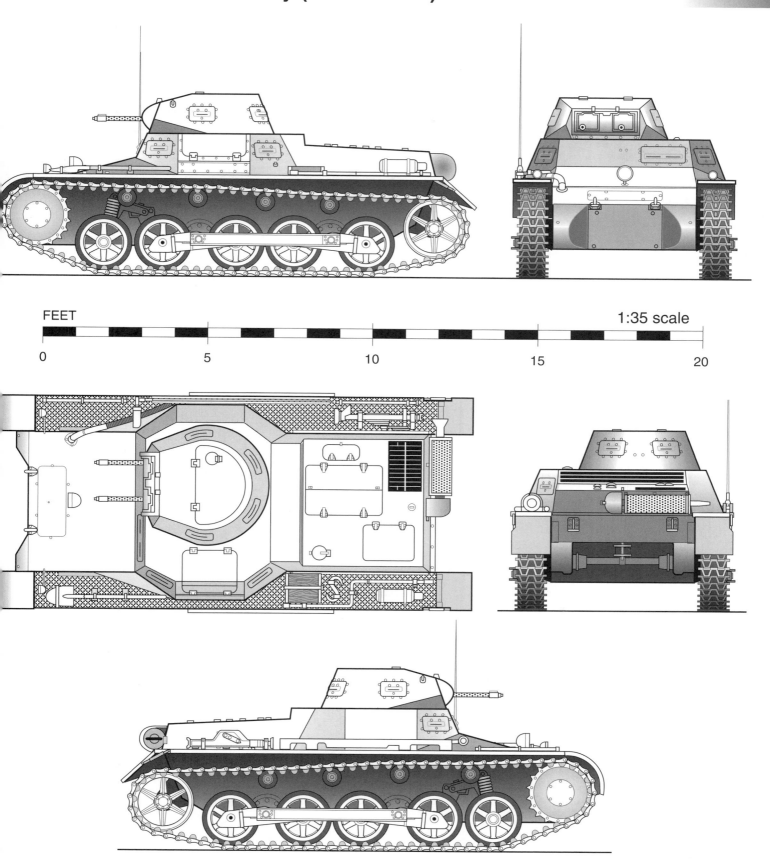

FEET

1:35 scale

0   5   10   15   20

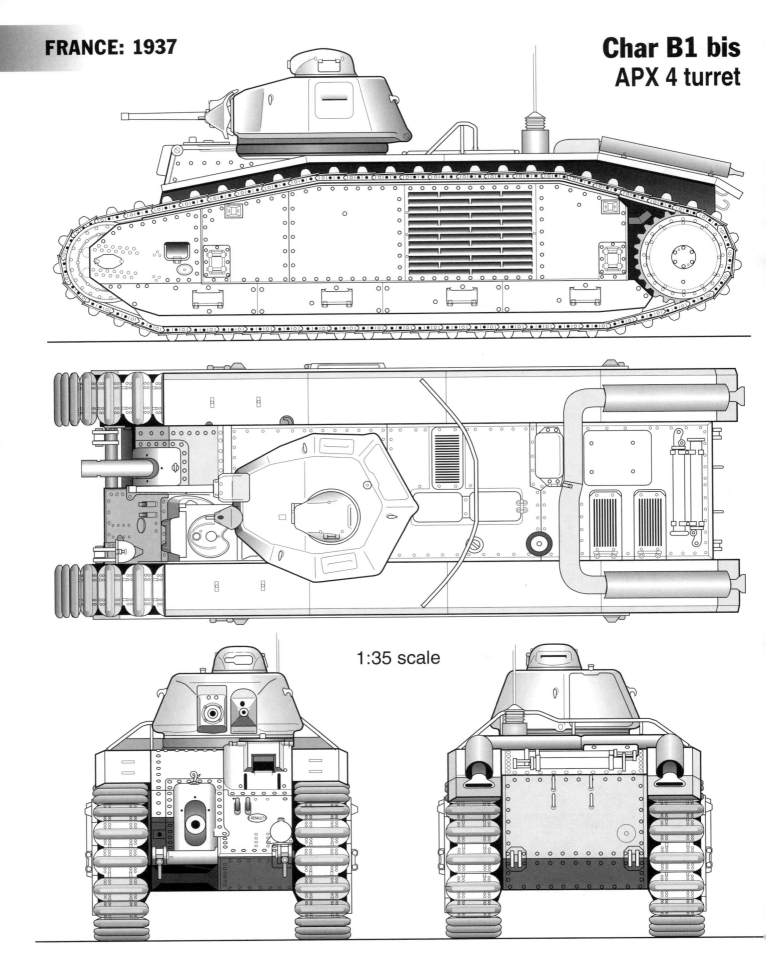

1:35 scale

Strv m/37 Light Tank
(Czech export of CKD tank AH-IV Sv)

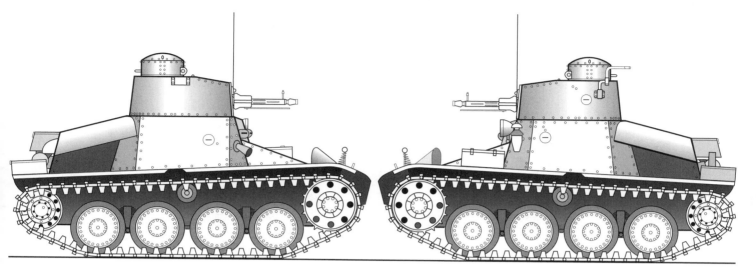

FEET

1:35 scale

0   5   10   15   20

Morris Recon
Light Armored Car
Model CS9/LAC

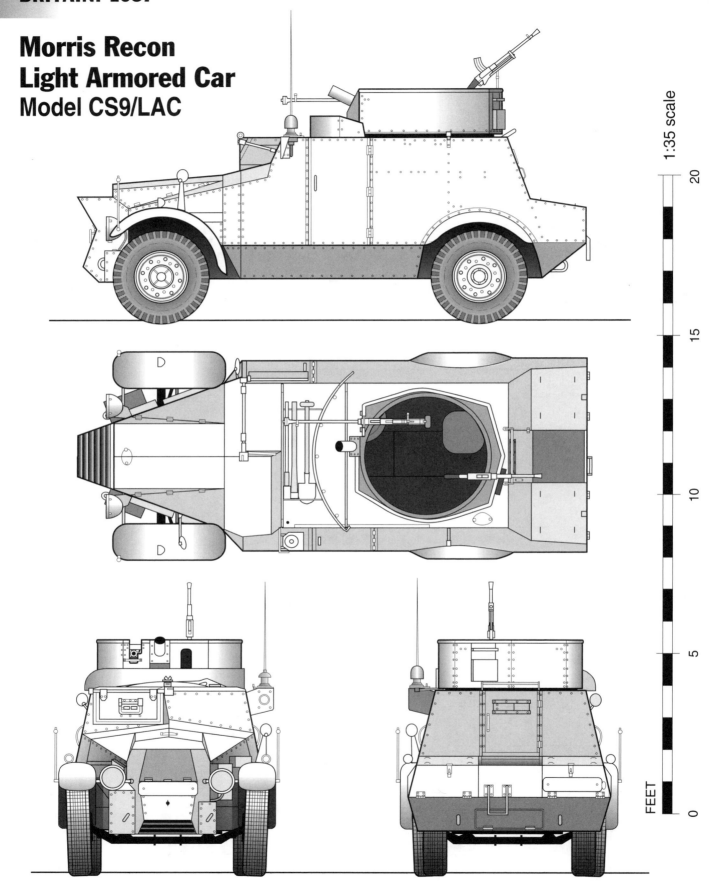

1:35 scale

FEET

T-26S Model 1937
Light Tank

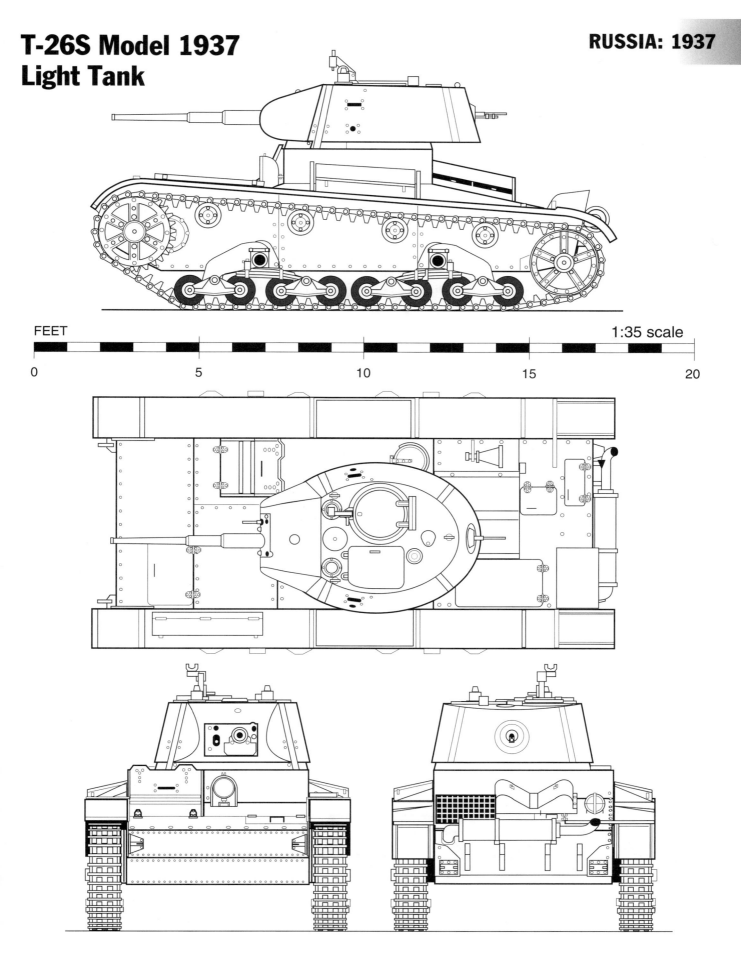

FEET

1:35 scale

0   5   10   15   20

Le véhicule blindé
Lorraine 1938L
de chasseurs portés
(Armored Infantry Carrier)

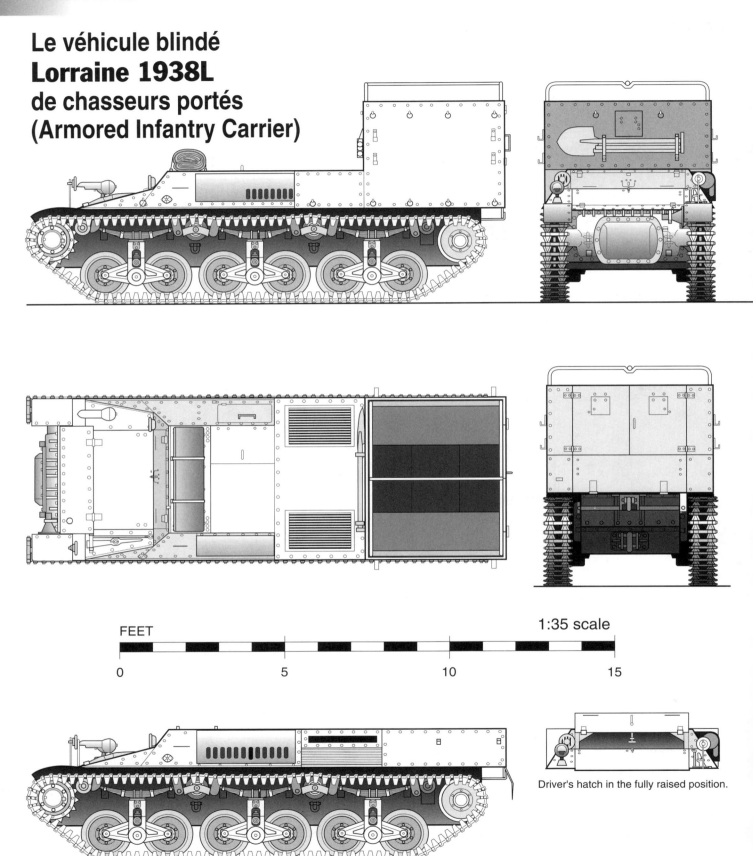

FEET

1:35 scale

0   5   10   15

Driver's hatch in the fully raised position.

Type 37 L Supply Vehicle (*tracteur de ravitaillement pour chars 1937 L*)

Pz.Kpfw. II Ausf. b
(Sd. Kfz. 121)

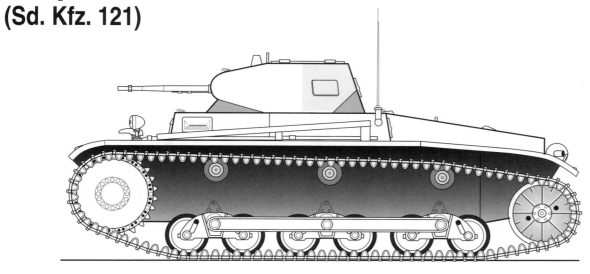

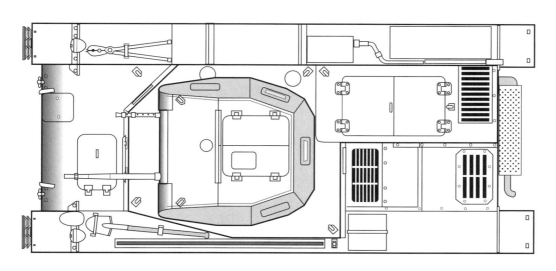

FEET

1:35 scale

0   5   10   15   20

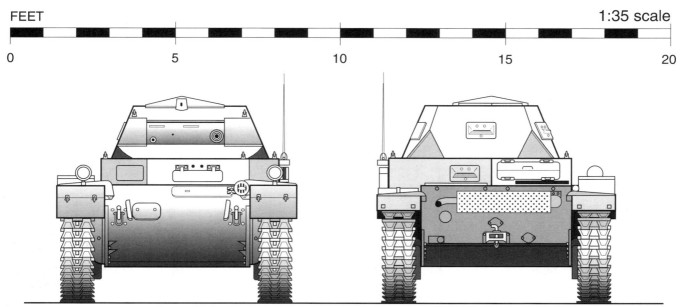

Pz.Kpfw. IV Ausf. A
(Sd. Kfz. 161)

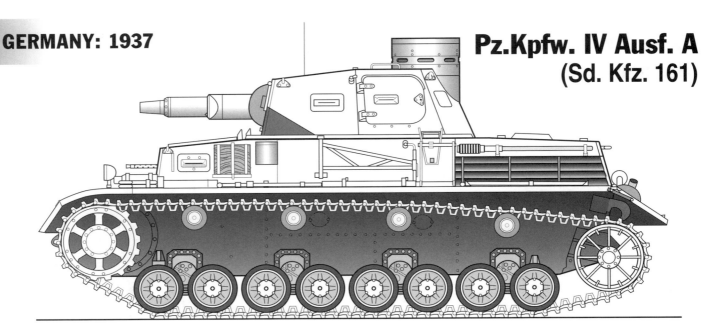

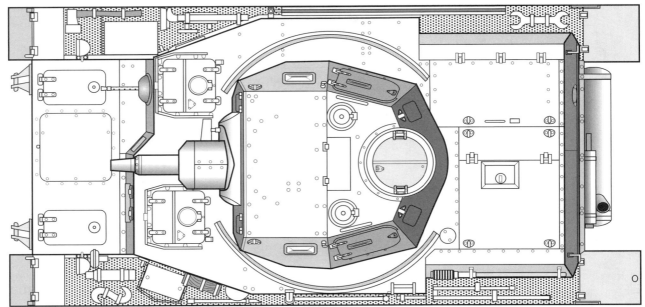

1:35 scale

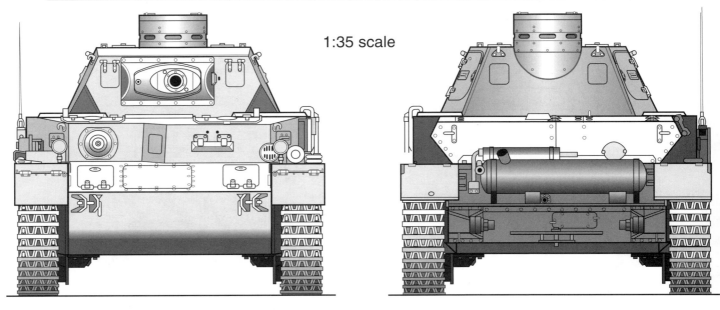

BT-7 Fast Tank
(Model 1937)

FEET

1:35 scale

0   5   10   15   20

M2 Combat Car
(Light Tank M1A1)

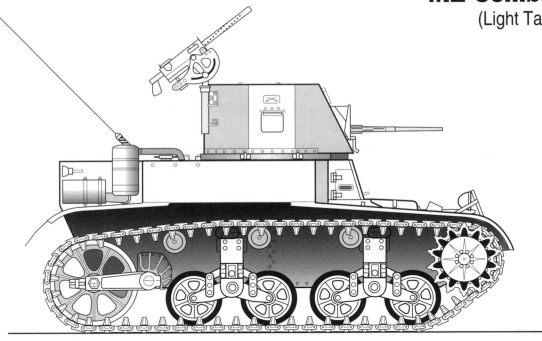

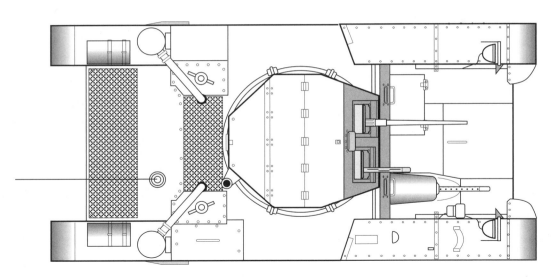

1:35 scale

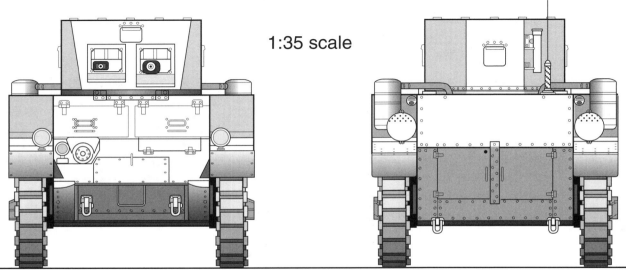

M2A2 Light Tank

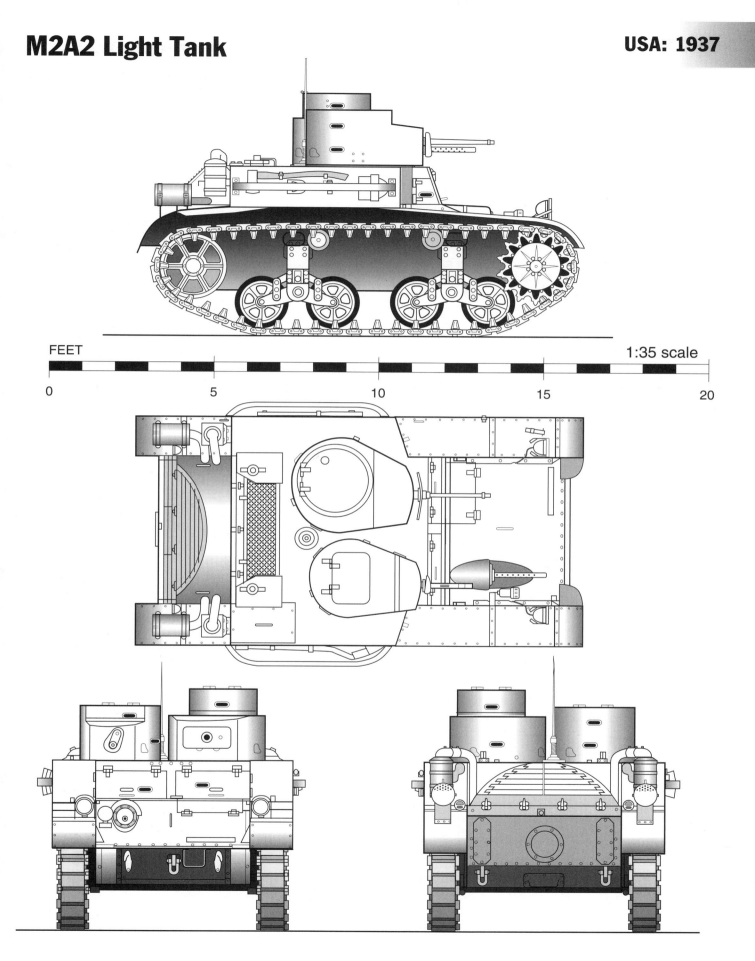

FEET

1:35 scale

0   5   10   15   20

Schwerer Panzerspähwagen
Sd.Kfz. 231 8-rad

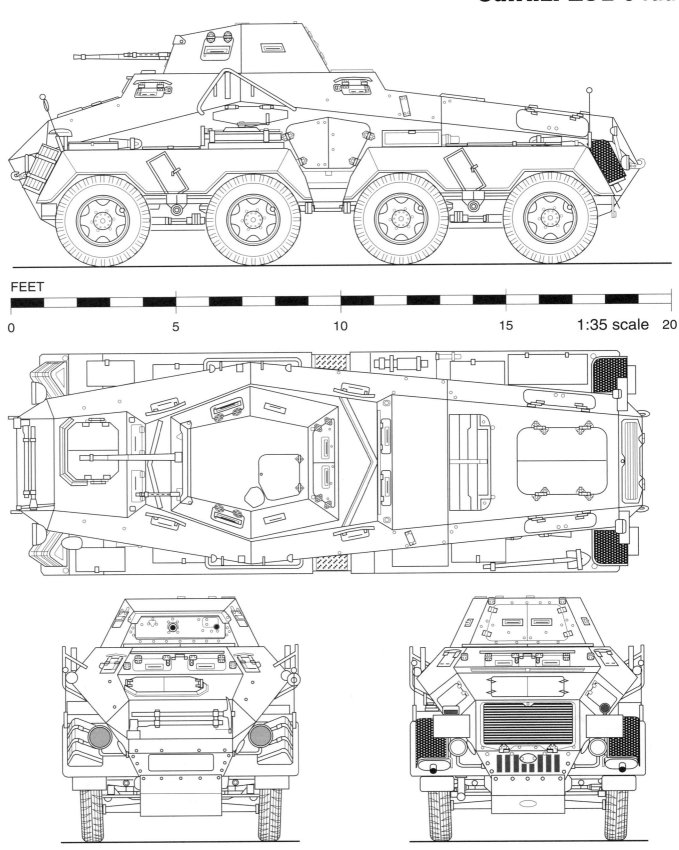

FEET

0   5   10   15   1:35 scale   20

Schwerer Panzerspähwagen
Sd.Kfz. 232 (Fu) 8-rad

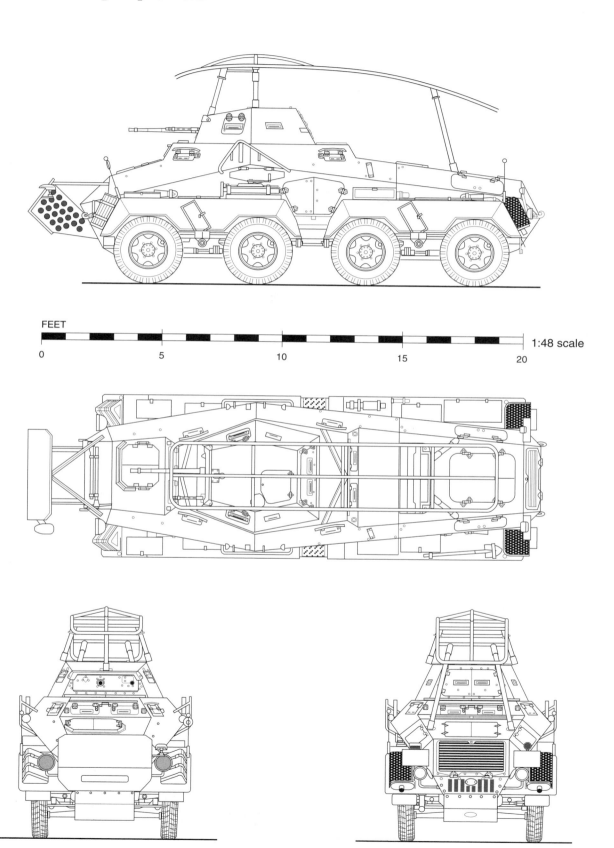

FEET

0   5   10   15   20

1:48 scale

Cruiser Tank Mark I
(A9)

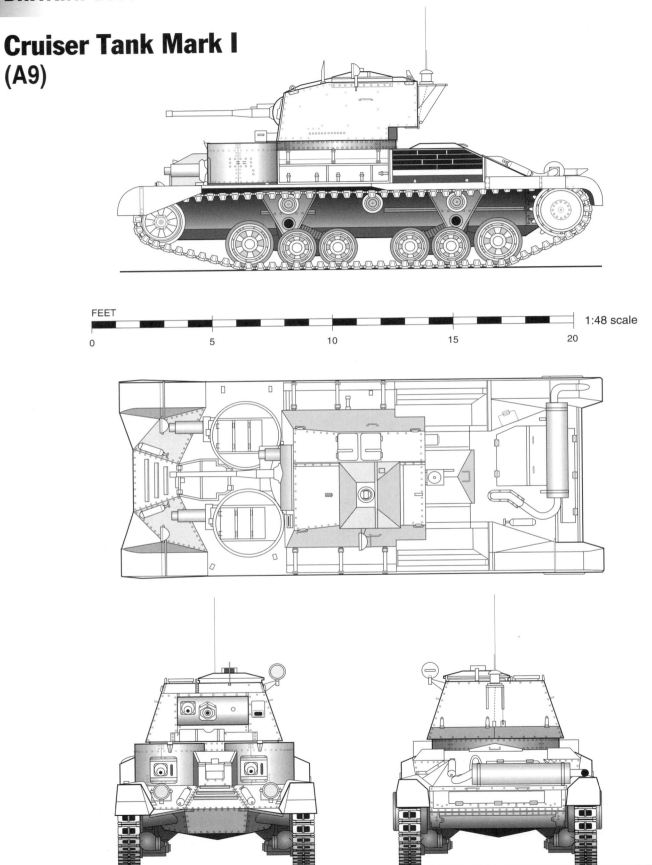

FEET

0   5   10   15   20

1:48 scale

7TPjw Light Tank

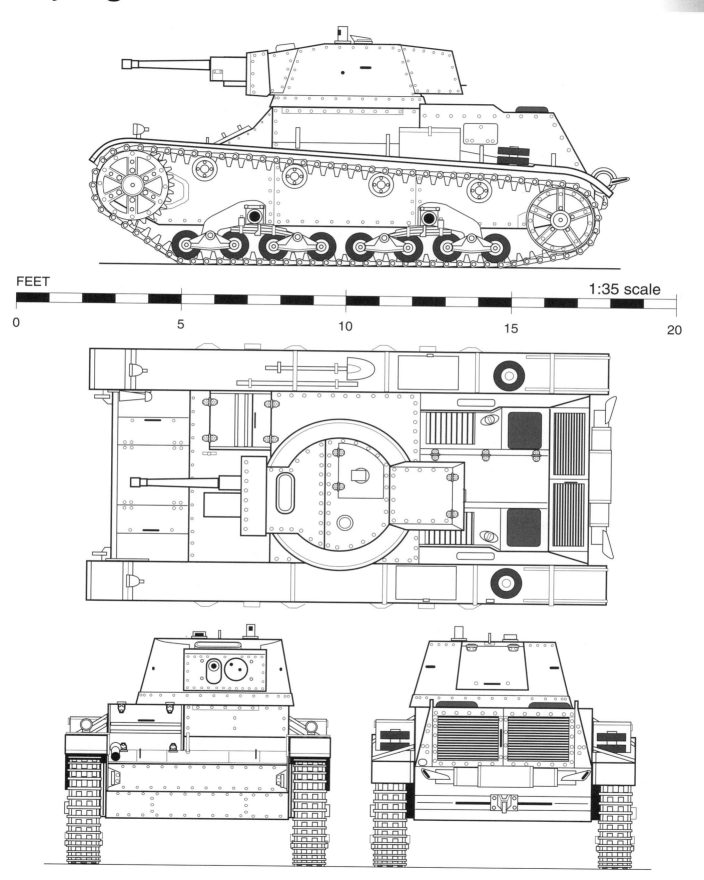

FEET

1:35 scale

0 5 10 15 20

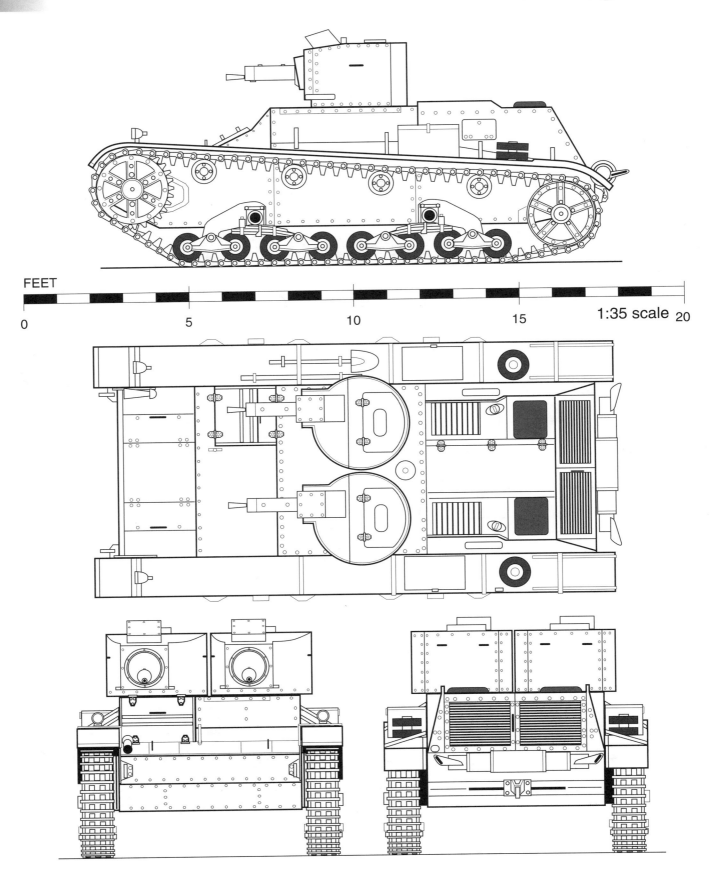

FEET

0   5   10   15   1:35 scale 20

Cruiser Tank Mark III
(A13 Mk. I)

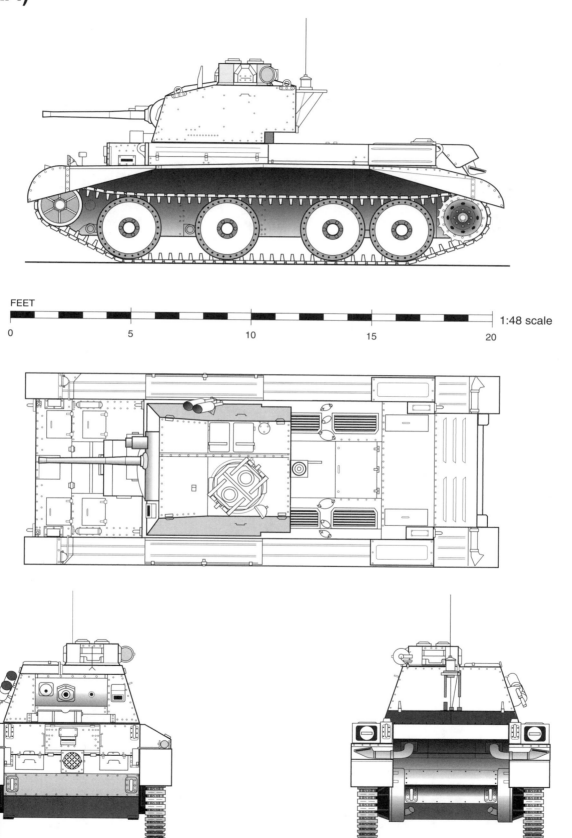

FEET

0   5   10   15   20

1:48 scale

SMK Heavy Tank
(Sergei Mironovich Kirov)

FEET

0   5   10   15   20

1:48 scale

Pantserwagen M.38 (L182)
6x4 Heavy Armored Car

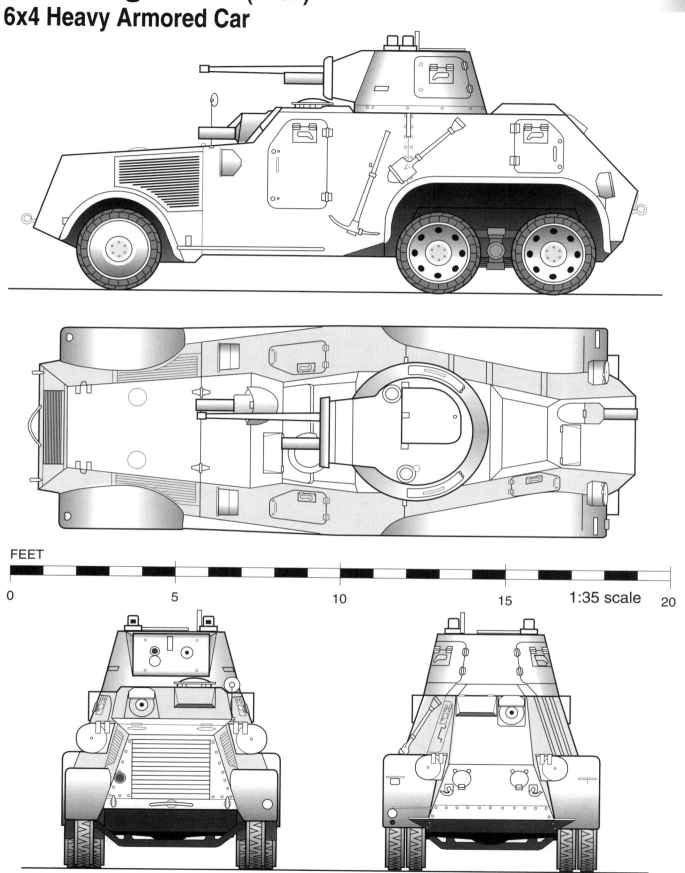

FEET

0   5   10   15   1:35 scale   20

Pantserwagen M.39
DAF Type 3 Heavy Armored Car

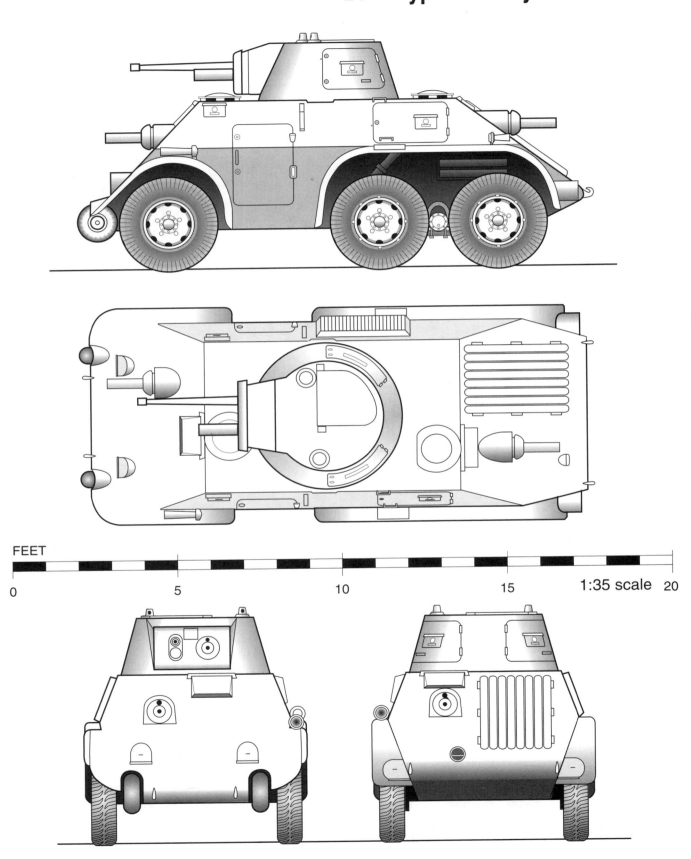

FEET

0   5   10   15   1:35 scale   20

M2A3 Light Tank

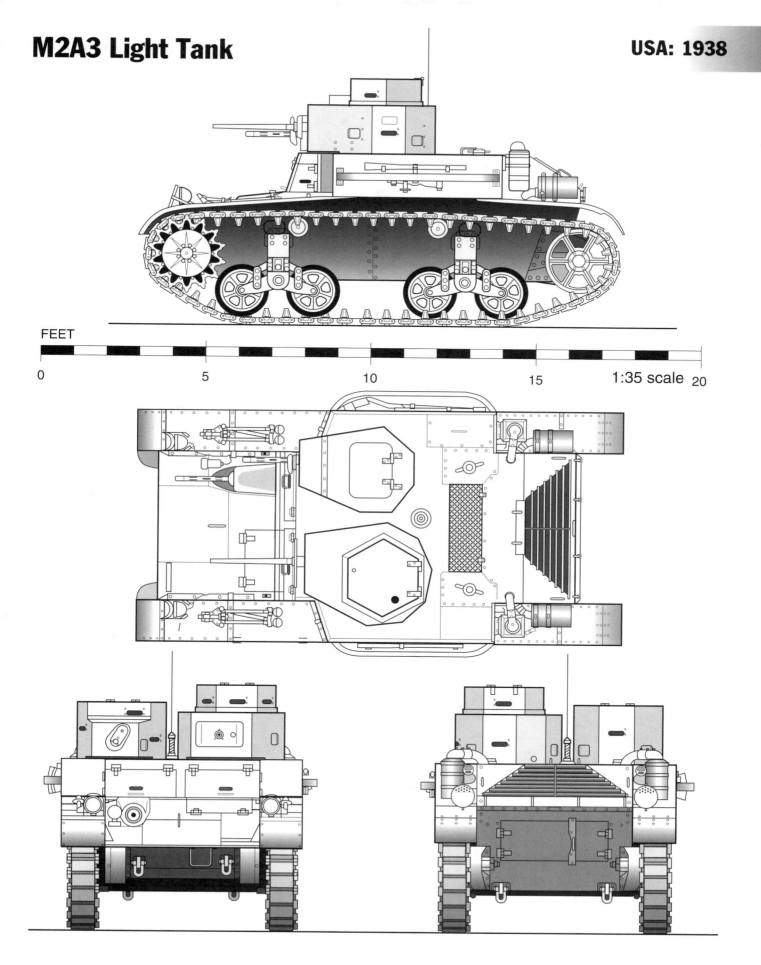

FEET

0 5 10 15 1:35 scale 20

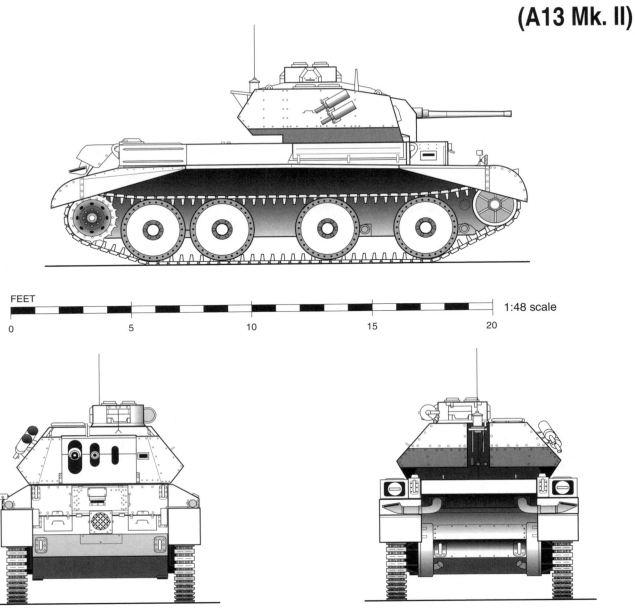

FEET

1:48 scale

0   5   10   15   20

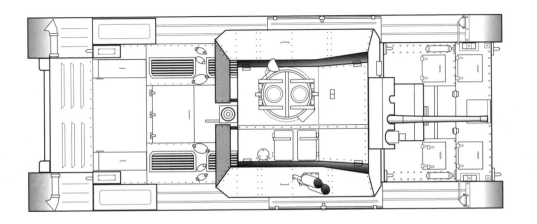

LT vz. 38 Light Tank
(TNH-P)

FEET

0   5   10   15   1:35 scale   20

Pz.Kpfw. II Ausf. C
(Sd. Kfz. 121)

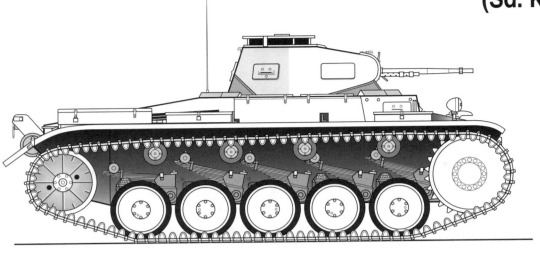

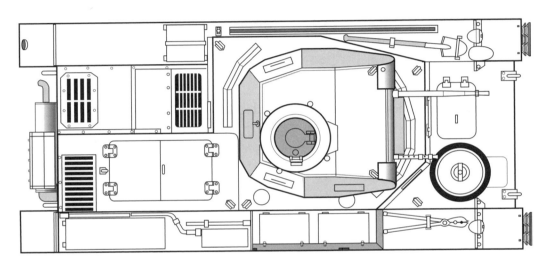

FEET
1:35 scale

0 5 10 15 20

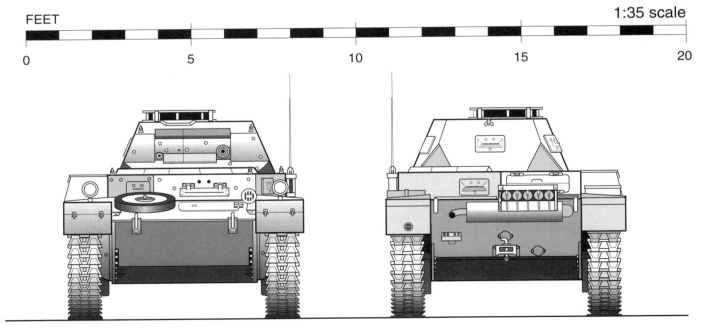

BIBLIOGRAPHY

Benvenuti, B.,
> *Carri Armati*, Vol. 1, Edizioni Bizzarri, Rome, Italy (1972)

Chamberlain, P.,
> *British & German Tanks of WWI*, Arms and Armour Press, London, UK (1969)
> *Tanks of The World 1915–45*, Arms and Armour Press, London, UK (1972)
> *Making Tracks: British Carrier Story*, Profile Publications Limited, Windsor, UK (1973)

Forty, G.,
> *A Photo History of Armoured Cars in Two World Wars*, Blandford Press, Poole, UK (1984)

Foss, C. F.,
> *The Encyclopedia of Tanks and Armoured Fighting Vehicles*, Amber Books Ltd., London, UK (2002)

Hunnicutt, R. P.,
> *Armored Car: A History of American Wheeled Combat Vehicles*, Presidio Press, Novato, CA, USA (2002)
> *Sherman: A History of the American Medium Tank*, Taurus Enterprises, Bellmont, CA, USA (1978)
> *Stuart: A History of the American Light Tank*, Presidio Press, Novato, CA, USA (1992)
> *Half-Track: A History of American Semi-Tracked Vehicles*, Presidio Press, Novato, CA, USA (2001)

Icks, Robert J.,
> *Tanks & Armored Vehicles 1900–1945*, We Inc., Old Greenwich, CT, USA
> *Encyclopedia of Tanks*, Barrie & Jenkins Limited, London, UK (1975)
> *Encyclopedia of Armoured Cars*, Chartwell Books Inc., Secaucus, NJ, USA (1976)

Jentz, T. L.,
> *Panzer Tracts No. 1–1, Panzerkampfwagen I: Kleintractor to Ausf.B*, Panzer Tracts, Boyds, MD, USA (2002)
> *Panzer Tracts No. 1–2, Panzerkampfwagen I: Kl.Pz.Bef.Wg to VK 18.01*, Panzer Tracts, Boyds, MD, USA (2002)
> *Panzer Tracts No. 13, Panzerspaehwagen, Sd.Kfz.3 to Sd.Kfz.263*, Panzer Tracts, Boyds, USA (2001)
> *Germany's Panzers from Pz.Kpfw.I to Tiger II*, Schiffer Publishing Ltd., Atglen, PA, USA (2001)

Jonca, A.,
> *Pojazdy Wojaska Polskiego, Barwa i bron*, Wydawnictwa Komunikacji i Lacznosci, Warsaw, Poland (1990)

Kliment, C. K.,
> *Czechoslovak Armored Fighting Vehicles 1918–1948*, Schiffer Publishing, Atglen, PA, USA (1997)

Lemon, C.,
> *Organization and Markings of United States Armored Units 1918–1941*, Schiffer Publishing Ltd., Atglen, PA, USA (2004)

Magnuski, J.,
> *Czerwony Blitzkrieg*, Pelta S.C., Warsaw, Poland (1994)

McNorgan, M.R.,
> *Great War Tanks in Canadian Service*, Service Publications, Ottawa, Ontario, Canada (2009)

Milsom, J.,
> *German Armoured Cars*, Arms and Armour Press, London, UK (1974)

Pignato, N.,
> *Dalla Libia Al Libano: 1912–1985*, Editrice Scorpione, Taranto, Italy (1992)

Pulsifer, C.,
> *The Armoured Autocar in Canadian Service*, Service Publications, Ottawa, Ontario, Canada (2007)

Touzin, P.,
> *Les Engins Blindés Français. 1920–1945*, Collections armes et uniformes, Sera, Paris, France (1976)
> *Les Véhicules Blindés Français, 1900–1944*, Editions E.P.A., Paris, France (1979)
> *Chars d'Assaut: French Battle Tanks*, Bellona Publications Ltd., Bracknell, Bershire, UK (1970)

White, B. T.,
> *British Tanks and Fighting Vehicles 1914–1945*, Ian Allan Ltd., Shepperton, Surrey, UK (1970)
> *British Tank Markings and Names*, Arms and Armour Press, London, UK (1978)
> *British Armoured Cars 1914–1945*, Ian Allan Ltd., Hampton Court, Surrey, UK
> *British Tanks 1915–1945*, Ian Allan Ltd., Hampton Court, Surrey, UK

Whitmore, M.,
> *Mephisto: A7V Sturpanzerwagen 506*, Queensland Museum, South Brisbane, Queensland, Australia (1989)

Zaloga, S. and J. Magnuski,
> *Soviet Tank and Combat Vehicles of World War Two*, Arms and Armour Press, London, UK (1984)

VARIOUS MODELING SCALES

Scale	1 inch equals	1 scale foot =	1 scale meter =	Comments
1:4	4"	3"	250.0 mm	Flying Models, Live-steam Trains
1:8	8"	$1^{1}/_{2}$"	125.0 mm	Cars, Motorocycles, Trains
1:12	1'	1"	83.3 mm	Cars, Motorcycles, Dollhouses
1:16	1' 4"	$^{3}/_{4}$"	62.5 mm	Cars, Motorcycles, Trains
1:20	1' 8"	$^{19}/_{32}$"	50.0 mm	Cars
1:22.5	1' $10^{1}/_{2}$"	$^{17}/_{32}$"	44.4 mm	G-Scale Trains
1:24	2'	$^{1}/_{2}$"	41.7 mm	Cars, Trucks, Dollhouses
1:25	2' 1"	$^{15}/_{32}$"	40.0 mm	Cars, Trucks
1:32	2' 8"	$^{3}/_{8}$"	31.25 mm	Aircraft, Cars, Tanks, Trains
1:35	2' 11"	$^{11}/_{32}$"	28.57 mm	Armor
1:43	3' 7"	$^{9}/_{32}$"	23.25 mm	Cars, Trucks
1:48	4'	$^{1}/_{4}$"	20.83 mm	Aircraft, Armor, O-Scale Trains
1:64	5' 4"	$^{3}/_{16}$"	15.62 mm	Aircraft, S-Scale Trains
1:72	6'	$^{11}/_{63}$"	13.88 mm	Aircraft, Armor, Boats
1:76	6' 4"	$^{5}/_{32}$"	13.16 mm	Armor
1:87	7' 3"	—	11.49 mm	Armor, HO-Scale Trains
1:96	8'	$^{1}/_{8}$"	10.42 mm	$^{1}/_{8}$" Scale Ships, Aircraft
1:100	8' 4"	—	10.00 mm	Aircraft
1:125	10' 5"	—	8.00 mm	Aircraft
1:144	12'	—	6.94 mm	Aircraft
1:160	13' 4"	—	6.25 mm	N-Scale Trains
1:192	16'	$^{1}/_{16}$"	5.21 mm	$^{1}/_{16}$" Scale Ships
1:200	16' 8"	—	5.00 mm	Aircraft, Ships

Stackpole Military History Series

THE AMERICAN CIVIL WAR
Cavalry Raids of the Civil War
Ghost, Thunderbolt, and Wizard
Pickett's Charge
Witness to Gettysburg

WORLD WAR I
Doughboy War

WORLD WAR II
After D-Day
Armor Battles of the Waffen-SS,
* 1943–45*
Armoured Guardsmen
Army of the West
Australian Commandos
The B-24 in China
Backwater War
The Battle of Sicily
Battle of the Bulge, Vol. 1
Battle of the Bulge, Vol. 2
Beyond the Beachhead
Beyond Stalingrad
Blitzkrieg Unleashed
Blossoming Silk against the Rising Sun
Bodenplatte
The Brandenburger Commandos
The Brigade
Bringing the Thunder
The Canadian Army and
* the Normandy Campaign*
Coast Watching in World War II
Colossal Cracks
Condor
A Dangerous Assignment
D-Day Bombers
D-Day Deception
D-Day to Berlin
Destination Normandy
Dive Bomber!
A Drop Too Many
Eagles of the Third Reich
The Early Battles of Eighth Army
Eastern Front Combat
Exit Rommel
Fist from the Sky
Flying American Combat Aircraft
* of World War II*
For Europe
Forging the Thunderbolt
For the Homeland

Fortress France
The German Defeat in the East,
* 1944–45*
German Order of Battle, Vol. 1
German Order of Battle, Vol. 2
German Order of Battle, Vol. 3
The Germans in Normandy
Germany's Panzer Arm in World War II
GI Ingenuity
Goodwood
The Great Ships
Grenadiers
Hitler's Nemesis
Infantry Aces
In the Fire of the Eastern Front
Iron Arm
Iron Knights
Kampfgruppe Peiper at the Battle
* of the Bulge*
The Key to the Bulge
Knight's Cross Panzers
Kursk
Luftwaffe Aces
Luftwaffe Fighter Ace
Luftwaffe Fighter-Bombers over Britain
Massacre at Tobruk
Mechanized Juggernaut or
* Military Anachronism?*
Messerschmitts over Sicily
Michael Wittmann, Vol. 1
Michael Wittmann, Vol. 2
Mountain Warriors
The Nazi Rocketeers
No Holding Back
On the Canal
Operation Mercury
Packs On!
Panzer Aces
Panzer Aces II
Panzer Aces III
Panzer Commanders of the
* Western Front*
Panzergrenadier Aces
Panzer Gunner
The Panzer Legions
Panzers in Normandy
Panzers in Winter
The Path to Blitzkrieg
Penalty Strike
Red Road from Stalingrad
Red Star under the Baltic
Retreat to the Reich

Rommel's Desert Commanders
Rommel's Desert War
Rommel's Lieutenants
The Savage Sky
Ship-Busters
The Siegfried Line
A Soldier in the Cockpit
Soviet Blitzkrieg
Stalin's Keys to Victory
Surviving Bataan and Beyond
T-34 in Action
Tank Tactics
Tigers in the Mud
Triumphant Fox
The 12th SS, Vol. 1
The 12th SS, Vol. 2
Twilight of the Gods
Typhoon Attack
The War against Rommel's Supply Lines
War in the Aegean
Wolfpack Warriors
Zhukov at the Oder

THE COLD WAR / VIETNAM
Cyclops in the Jungle
Expendable Warriors
Flying American Combat Aircraft:
* The Cold War*
Here There Are Tigers
Land with No Sun
MiGs over North Vietnam
Phantom Reflections
Street without Joy
Through the Valley

WARS OF AFRICA AND THE MIDDLE EAST
Never-Ending Conflict
The Rhodesian War

GENERAL MILITARY HISTORY
Carriers in Combat
Cavalry from Hoof to Track
Desert Battles
Guerrilla Warfare
Ranger Dawn
Sieges

Real Battles. Real Soldiers. Real Stories.